AN ACCIDENTAL ENVOY

First published in 2021 by Puxley Productions Ltd..

Copyright © 2021 by Bill Samuel.

All rights reserved.

No part of this document may be reproduced or transmitted in any form or by any means, electronic, mechanical, photocopying, recording, or otherwise, without prior written permission of the copyright owner.

This is a work of nonfiction. Any similarity between the characters and situations within its pages, and places, persons, or animals living or dead, could be unintentional and co-incidental. Some names and identifying details have been changed or omitted to, in part, protect the privacy of individuals.

The right of Bill Samuel to be identified as the author of this work has been asserted by him in accordance with sections 77 and 78 of the Copyright, Designs and Patents Act, 1988.

British Library Cataloguing in Publication Data.
A catalogue record for this book is available from the British Library.

ISBN: 978-1-9160782-4-6 (hardback)

Typeset in Berling
Printed and bound by Ingram Spark in the UK.

Cover Design and typesetting by Jamie Keenan.

Also by Bill Samuel

AN ACCIDENTAL BOOKSELLER
A personal memoir of Foyles

www.billsamuel.co.uk
@booksellerbill

AN ACCIDENTAL ENVOY

A Personal Memoir of
The Turks and Caicos Islands

BILL SAMUEL

CAÏCOS PASSAGE

THREE MARY CAYS
Sandy Point
PARROT CAY
Whitby
NORTH CAÏCOS
Kew
MAJOR HILL CAY
DELLIS CAY
FT. GEORGE CAY
PINE CAY
STUBBS CAY
WATER CAY
LITTLE WATER CAY
DONNA CAY
Blue Hills settlements
The Bright Settlements
MANGROVE CAY
Chalk Sound
PROVIDENCIALES
FIVE CAYS

WEST CAÏCOS

Southwest Reefs

21° 30

Molasses Reefs

FRENCH CAY

WEST SAND SPIT

HAÏTI

STROMBUS

Turks & Caïcos Islands

Discovered 1512 by J. Ponce de Leon
Bermudian 1678 — Spanish 1710 —
British 1766 — French 1783 —

Settled 1784 by Georgia Loyalists

NORTH ATLANTIC OCEAN

- Dickish Cay
- Joe Grant's Cay
- Iguana Cay
- Philips Reef
- East Caïcos
- Hog Cay
- Nigger Cay
- Big Cameron Cay
- Middle Creek Cay
- Plandon Cay
- Sail Rock Island
- South Caïcos
- Cockburn Harbour
- Middleton Cay
- Six Hill Cays
- Long Cay
- Grand Turk
- Cockburn Town
- Gibbs Cay
- Long Cay
- Penniston Cay
- Cotton Cay
- Pear Cay
- East Cay
- Fish Cays
- Balfour Town
- Salt Cay
- Big Ambergris Cay
- Bush Cay
- Big Sand Cay
- Mouchoir Passage
- Pear Cay
- Endymion Rock
- Hot Cay
- Whale Breaker
- Swimmer Rock
- South Rock

Contents

1. From One Small Island To Another 1
2. Setting the scene 7
3. Dramatis personae 17
4. The Mokoro Strategic Review 23
5. The Tourist Board 49
6. The Offshore Finance Centre 75
7. Development 91
8. Morning Commute 101
9. Island Life 107
10. Whales, Dolphins and Other Fishy Things .. 127
11. Their Man in London 141
12. Lessons learned 157
    Postscript 162
    Acknowledgements 164

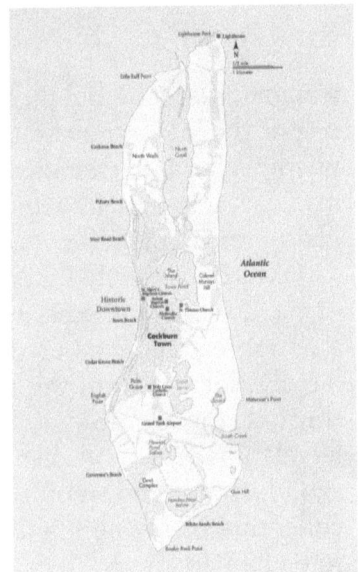

1. FROM ONE SMALL ISLAND TO ANOTHER

IT WAS A SLEEPY SUNDAY afternoon in September 1990. Life, as is its wont, had dealt me a couple of bad hands after a four-year winning streak and my soul was bruised. I stood on a hotel balcony, the sea in front of me turquoise, shading to navy out towards the western horizon. The beach itself was golden sand with small outcroppings of coral rock, the air heavy and still and the sea barely moving, just the occasional ripple of a wave limping inconsequentially a few inches up the beach, only to give up and return to the languid ocean. To the right some casuarinas gave definition to the scene and in the distance an osprey perched on a telecommunication tower, scanning the sea for fish. To the left a few ramshackle bungalows squatted behind white stone walls, scant protection from the sea in harsher weather. The temperature was thirty degrees, it was mid-afternoon and there was not a soul in sight. From one of the lowest points in my life, forty-nine years old, unemployed and unemployable, heavily in debt and with my 26-year marriage beginning to disintegrate I thought I had arrived in paradise.

More accurately I was in Grand Turk, capital island of the Turks and Caicos, a small tropical archipelago of a nation on the edge of the Atlantic. Grand Turk was largely isolated from the world, observing the outside through the window of television but leading a life largely unaffected by changes elsewhere. A few months ago I had only known of its existence through the stamp collection of my childhood: a few months later I was to be its Director of Tourism. My first visit of six weeks developed into a long term relationship that has given me great pleasure, a lot of fun, some minor heartaches and many wonderful memories. Those memories are already beginning to jumble and I will not attempt to try to force them back into strict chronological order - I do not want to paint a static portrait or write a journal; this is a memoir of my relationship with a living and vibrant community. I write as an outsider, an observer, but for a time I was also a participant.

* * *

In the space of half a year I had gone from one small island, awash with the late twentieth century oil wealth of the Arabian Gulf to another, on the other side of the world in the Caribbean, still living largely in the late nineteenth century. I had for a few years been working in Bahrain, an executive director of a major Arab-owned investment bank, with a large modern house in a gated compound, its high, echoing rooms air-conditioned to sterile coldness, equipped with all the modern conveniences money could buy. My daily commute was a 10 minute drive beside the sea in an air-conditioned car to an air-conditioned office in the heart of Manama, the continuity of the air-conditioning insulating me from the sometimes harsh realities of the Gulf climate.

I had known the bank's CEO, a charismatic Iraqi banker, for almost a decade. He had been introduced to me by a lawyer in Bahrain and had sought my advice on the appropriate corporate structure for the unique institution he wanted to create; in the intervening years I met with him from time to time and eventually, with my own business going nowhere he had persuaded me to join the management team of what was becoming a very respected financial institution.

Towards the end of December 1989 he asked me to come to the London office for a marketing meeting, which I was more than happy to do as it gave me the opportunity to spend Christmas with my daughters at our home in Surrey. My wife, my youngest daughter Emma and I flew back from Bahrain in the comfort of Cathay Pacific's first class cabin, to which I had become accustomed, and the following morning I duly presented myself at the beautiful eighteenth century building in Mayfair's Brook Street which was the bank's London office. I had a chat with some of the staff who I knew well, having worked with them in London for a couple of years before transferring to Bahrain; there was a festive atmosphere and I was relaxed, in a Christmas mood, quite unprepared for the body blow I was about to get.

I was a little surprised on entering his beautifully-furnished office to see that the other two members of the marketing committee weren't there but I sat down and accepted the coffee he offered. He then went on to tell me the real reason I had been asked to return to London: in the annual appraisal process the judgement given by my peers was that I didn't really belong in the organisation as

I was not sufficiently 'corporate'. Of course, I could have told them that when I was recruited four years earlier had they but asked. So without warning my extraordinarily well-paid employment was terminated with immediate effect and at the age of 48 I found myself unemployed and, as I soon realised, effectively unemployable.

Once I got over the initial shock we discussed the terms under which I would leave and although I hadn't completed the requisite 5 years' service the CEO agreed that I could still have the value of my stock options which had been a substantial part of my remuneration package. He asked me to type up a brief document summarising our agreement, which I immediately did and which he signed. After a rather subdued family Christmas we flew back to Bahrain to wind up our affairs – we had a fully furnished house and Emma was in school there. The CEO asked me to calculate the value of the stock options and give the figure to his secretary so she could arrange payment; this I did, the figure was substantial, enough to fund a comfortable retirement. Shortly afterwards I received a phone call from the CEO saying that he couldn't possibly pay that amount to someone who had effectively been dismissed. I had, for the record, been recruited nearly four years earlier specifically to develop the funds management department which at the time was managing a paltry $17m with a staff of three. By the time I left we had increased that figure to just short of $1bn, there were four staff and the department was generating some $5m annual profits, so I had no difficulty in justifying to myself the amount due to me. But justifying the claim didn't put money into my bank account and the legal process to enforce the signed agreement was likely to be long so, just short of my half-century, having been abroad or self-employed for most of my working life I had to find gainful employment.

I decided to fall back on my professional qualification – I am a Chartered Accountant - and applied for any suitable accounting jobs, to be told time and time again that I was over-qualified. I networked far and wide and eventually a friend introduced me to a consultancy group based near Oxford which had its origins in development work in Southern Africa, taking its name Mokoro from the Botswanan dugout canoe widely used in the beautiful wetlands of the Okavango Delta. Unlike most consultancy firms Mokoro was established as a not-for-profit organisation; it had an enviable reputation for producing studies and proposals designed to bring about effective change. I met with them, was immediately attracted to the company and its ethos, but was told that, unfortunately, they had nothing in their pipeline of work requiring my particular private sector commercial experience, nor did they expect to have anything in the foreseeable future.

But serendipity is real and it was a very pleasant surprise, and a great relief, when they called me the following day to say that they possibly had a role for me. They had, that morning, received from the Overseas Development Administration an invitation to tender for a major strategic review of the economy of the Turks and Caicos Islands and one of the requirements was that the team include someone with private sector experience and in particular with expertise in both tourism and financial services. Both these sectors were outside their usual areas of expertise and I seemed to be ideally qualified for the job; a few weeks later, from one of the lowest points of my life, unemployed and deeply in debt, I found myself heading for a remote tropical island in the Caribbean.

I had absolutely no idea that this would lead to a 15-year enjoyable and fulfilling relationship with a tiny nation of which I had hardly heard, but life does that sort of thing, doesn't it?

2. SETTING THE SCENE

SANDWICHED BETWEEN THE WILD ATLANTIC and the generally more docile Caribbean, some 600 miles south east of Miami, lies the tiny and little known nation of the Turks and Caicos Islands. TCI comprises two small archipelagos, separated geographically by a two-thousand-metre deep and 20 mile wide marine trench, and culturally by very different ambitions. To the east are the Turks Islands, low-lying and rocky, their stark and ocean-battered landscape in total contrast to the underwater beauty of the coral reefs which surround them. The Caicos Islands in the west are geologically an extension of the Bahamas, an inverted crescent embracing 50 miles of shallow coral banks, the sea never more than a few metres deep, home to a wonderfully diverse marine life including turtle-nurseries and large shoals of bone fish, almost inedible but much prized by fisherman for their fighting spirit. The outside of the crescent is endless miles of the finest white coral sand beaches in the Caribbean. The trade winds which brought Christopher Columbus from Europe sweep in from the Atlantic and are deflected upwards by the low cliffs of Grand Turk, cooling just enough to deposit some of their moisture as rain on the more fertile Caicos Islands.

For many centuries the tides of history have washed back and forth over these islands, gradually depositing the silt that makes up their unique culture: At various times they have been nominally ruled by the Spaniards, the French and the British, and administered by Bermuda, the Bahamas and Jamaica. In the early 18th century they were a refuge for pirates; they were later settled by merchants from Bermuda who established a salt industry and loyalists fleeing North America after the war of independence in 1774 who tried to establish plantations. They are now peopled by a mixed race descended from these various groups of settlers and the slaves they all brought with them. It is little wonder that Turks Islanders have over the years struggled to find their identity.

The 300 year governance of the islands directly or indirectly by the British has been, from the start, characterised by benign neglect. The neglect was benign only in that it was not ill-intentioned; there was nothing particularly benevolent in the relationship. For a couple of centuries little was done to develop the islands and it is doubtful that it would have occurred to anyone in the Colonial Office in London that any development might have been beneficial to the local inhabitants. The islands were far from London with neither agriculture nor minerals to attract the attention of their distant rulers. On the Turks Islands Bermudians and their light-skinned but increasingly mixed-race descendants continued to ship salt, raked from the salinas by the darker-skinned descendants of their slaves. On the Caicos Islands the descendants of the slaves abandoned by the loyalists when plantations were found to be unviable became fishermen, supplementing the rich harvest of the Caicos Banks with subsistence farming.

The British established their administrative headquarters on Grand Turk which, with the salt industry, had the only significant commercial activity. In the 1960s a few intrepid expatriates, mainly from North America, began visiting Providenciales, one of the Caicos islands, home to a few hundred fishermen. Possibly attracted by the almost complete absence of any authority they began to settle, unobtrusively and largely ignored by Grand Turk. Rather than shoulder the burden of infrastructure development the administration sold, to a group of these expatriates, 6000 acres of prime government-owned land for $1 per acre, on the condition they put in the basic infrastructure. They fulfilled the easy part of this very attractive deal by putting in a basic airstrip and marina. It would be nice to think that giving away 6000 acres of the finest development land in the Caribbean was part of some clever masterplan but my experience of British colonial administration makes me doubt it.

It was nearly 20 years after the this deal that the British Government, under pressure from both the UN Decolonization Committee and its own parliament, made an attempt to kick-start the economy into self-sufficiency and hopefully enable the UK to rid itself of the burden of this very financially dependent territory. They built on Providenciales an airport and a road running east along the spine of the island, the grandly-named Leeward Highway. Both were decidedly underspecified, shoddily built down to a budget; a four wheel drive vehicle was needed for much of the 'highway' and the airport consultants brought in after completion to check the runway found that there was a serious risk of a large passenger jet ploughing through the surface and causing a catastrophic accident. The UK's major concern with its Overseas Territories was - and remains – any contingent risk for which Her Majesty's Government, HMG, might be liable. After the consultants' findings HMG, concerned by the prospect of a multi-billion dollar lawsuit from well-off Americans, had the runway rebuilt at breakneck speed and at a cost of some $10 million.

At the same time a 70 acre plot of prime beachfront land was given to Club Med, the French operator of all-inclusive holiday resorts. For predictable reasons this didn't have the economic impact which had been expected. Club Med brought in its own construction workers and operating staff and actively discouraged its tourists from leaving the resort or using any outside services so the benefit to the economy was small while the damage to the environment, particularly to the coral reefs from Club Med's rather buccaneering approach to diving, was not inconsiderable.

In the meantime with government revenues almost nil and little prospect of work for Turks Islanders apart from in the civil service, some gentlemen from South America took to visiting the islands in their light aircraft for unofficial nocturnal refuelling stops to which the then Chief Minister turned a blind eye. This did not go unnoticed and the always-uneasy relationship between London and TCI was not improved when, in 1985, the Chief Minister was arrested in Miami on drug-related conspiracy charges: he was subsequently sentenced to eight years imprisonment. HMG commissioned a review of the governance of the islands by the prominent QC Louis Blom Cooper who commented that most of the local politicians were unfit to hold public office and should be removed. As he so eloquently put it, 'I am driven to the conclusion that the time has come to disperse the cloud that hangs like an omnipresence in a Grand Turkan sky.' 'Dispersing the cloud' was a fine ambition, but for a while HMG's actions were unequal to the rhetoric of its Queen's Counsel.

* * *

There are some thirty-five islands in the Turks and Caicos, of which six are inhabited. It is one of the last remaining British Dependent Territories, renamed in 2002 the UK Overseas Territories, a purely cosmetic change made by the Mother Country as it continued to tidy up some of the lingering embarrassments of its colonial past, suggesting a change of status without actually conferring it. Constitutionally Her Majesty's Government is responsible for governance and foreign affairs, appointing the Governor, Attorney General, Finance Secretary and Chief Secretary, as the head of the civil service was known;

the local elected government is responsible for all domestic affairs, although as all civil service employment is handled by the Chief Secretary's office the British are still able to influence most appointments.

In 1990 the economy was based largely on fishing, mainly for conch and marine crayfish (usually inaccurately called lobster) exported to the US, tourism-with a few hundred hotel rooms spread across all the islands- and financial services, in which they lagged about 15 years behind the Cayman Islands. It ran at a deficit of many millions of dollars a year (the country uses the US dollar as its currency) and was heavily subsidised by the UK. The total population of the islands was 12000 which, to put this tiny nation into perspective, is approximately the same as that of Buckingham, now my local market town in the UK. Of those, fewer than 4000 lived on the capital island of Grand Turk with most of those of working age being employed in government service. The embryonic tourism industry was centred on Providenciales, by then the most populous island, home to another 5000, about half of whom were expatriates, North Americans and Europeans at one end of the social scale, Haitians and those from the Dominican Republic at the other.

Grand Turk is a tiny speck of coral limestone some six miles long and two miles across at its widest, oriented north to south. Much of its area is water, with North Creek, an inviting-looking anchorage made dangerous by the razor-sharp coral reefs guarding its entrance, dividing the top third into two high and narrow spits of land; a chain of salinas, salt ponds, is scattered around the middle, reaching down to South Creek, marshy and malodorous with a richness of birdlife. Two thirds of the way down the island the runway of the small airport runs from coast to coast; much of the land south of the runway is empty scrub, grazing for the horses, mules and feral donkeys, left over from the old salt-raking operations.

At each end of the island are the remains of two military bases built by America in the 1950s. North Base, overlooked by a nineteenth century lighthouse and now largely abandoned, was once a link in the chain of cold-war sound surveillance systems operated by the US Navy; South Base, set up as an Airforce missile tracking facility and the first landfall of John Glenn after his historic orbit of the earth, is now home to much of the civil service.

Most of the inhabitants live in the couple of square miles between North Creek and the airport, in single story dwellings of whitewashed coral limestone blocks with small, dusty gardens strung along a fairly haphazard network of roads between the salinas and the sea. Halfway up the island on the west side is Cockburn Town, named after the British admiral prominent in the Caribbean during the Napoleonic wars; the name is shown on maps but I have never heard it used on the island – the town is simply 'town'.

Town is a collection of mainly nineteenth century buildings straggling inland from the waterfront where ancient cannons, relics from a time when the Caribbean was the least law-abiding part of the world, are still trained out to sea and the bones of a few small vessels which came to grief on the reefs stick up through the sand in which they found their graves; it is home to Government offices, some of the churches, a couple of banks and two or three grandly-styled supermarkets offering a limited selection of food and drink.

The British Governor keeps his distance, metaphorically and physically, at Waterloo, his official home roughly midway between town and South Base. Waterloo is a beautiful old house built of stone and cedar, set in a grove of casuarinas on the edge of a golden sand beach, for me far nicer than the shining white beaches of Providenciales. As is apparent from its name Waterloo was built in 1815, by James Misick, a Bermudan salt merchant; my friend Washington Misick is a descendant of one of his slaves and I have often thought it would be some sort of justice if Washy had become the first native governor, taking up residence where once his ancestor had been a slave. It was, of course, not to be – the Misicks are not high on HMG's list of favourite people, some because they are too smart for the average colonial administrator, one because the corruption he introduced was far too open – the British prefer their corruption to be rather more subtle; there is however the kernel of a historical novel in there somewhere.

* * *

In the UK Overseas territories if there is a perceived lack of expertise in the local population the available skills are augmented by Technical Cooperation Officers (TCOs) sent out by the Department for International Development, as the Overseas Development Authority is now known, as part of the UK's programme of aid. In 1990 there were about 30 TCOs on Grand Turk, involved in everything from fisheries to public health. Many of them moved from territory to territory, their salaries augmented by substantial tax free allowances, serving their time while doing little to transfer their skills to the locals. Their working hours were officially 8 till 4.30 with an hour for lunch but for many of them punctuality was only for the locals, their work/life balance was weighted towards life and their hours were flexed to favour the leisure side, particularly at lunchtime. It is fair to say that with one or two outstanding exceptions, TCOs were understandably not held in high regard by the natives. The antipathy was mutual: Within the TCO community the islands were sometimes referred to as 'Turds and Chaos'.

Most of the TCOs reported to the British Development Division in the Caribbean, BDDC, the Barbados office of the ODA, imposing an additional layer of bureaucracy between those few who wished to implement change and the ultimate decision takers in London. Communication was through the desk officer who made himself very elusive; he was eventually reprimanded and retired under a cloud, a subsequent investigation finding that he travelled for more than 200 days a year in his last couple of years, frequently overnighting in Miami and pocketing several hundred dollars a night in subsistence payments whilst staying in the cheapest of hotels.

The distain exhibited by Whitehall is exemplified by the history of TCI's flag. I have one in my house, left over from my time as the official UK representative of the Islands' Government. It has a union jack in the top left hand corner and on the right a shield decorated with three symbols of the islands: a conch, a crayfish and a Turks head cactus. It isn't a thing of beauty but it does at least symbolise the islands which its precursor did not. Towards the end of the nineteenth century, while the islands were still a dependency of Jamaica, they argued for having their own flag. As a basis for the design the Colonial Office sent to the Admiralty a copy of the seal of the islands which had a foreground representing salt heaps with a rake and in the background a three-masted ship about to set sail. The draftsman, not bothering to do any research on this unimportant and distant little British possession the location of which was not of interest to him, interpreted the white mounds of salt incorrectly so for the next 80 years these small tropical islands had on their flag a couple of igloos. This lack of interest in or commitment to its overseas territories persists in London to this day.

By the end of the 1980s the governance of the islands, still recovering from the Norman Saunders drug scandal, was in uneasy stasis, benign neglect of the colonial rulers versus the demanding incompetence of the local government.

This then was the Turks and Caicos Islands where I arrived on that Sunday in the September of 1990.

3. DRAMATIS PERSONAE

MOST OF HISTORY IS THE result of apparently unconnected coincidences and the fortuitous happenings which brought three people with very different backgrounds into positions of influence in this small nation at the same time was, I believe, a major factor in bringing about the changes needed to propel the country forward.

Washington Misick, known to all as Washy, is the oldest of 12 children born to an ambitious mother who wanted more for her children than the life of fishing which the family had followed on North Caicos for generations, since their ancestors were brought to the islands as slaves in the eighteenth century. He studied accountancy and after working for a while in Jamaica returned to TCI and established a successful real estate business. His siblings included two lawyers, a doctor, an engineer and a real estate developer – there are strong genes in the family. Eventually, frustrated by the inability of the local politicians to be other than confrontational towards the British and from his real estate business seeing that top-end tourism offered the opportunity to lift the islands out of dependency he entered politics and by 1990 was the leader of the opposition. Charming, thoughtful and understated he had a good strategic mind and the powerful presence necessary to be an effective political leader.

Richard Stoneman, who was to become, and remains, a good friend, is an economist with an exceptionally fine mind and the ability to view things holistically and to think outside the box. He had spent the early years of his career as a development economist with the UK government, including a three year posting in his mid-20s to the BDDC where he was responsible for major financial and economic decisions in newly-independent Caribbean islands. He became increasingly aware of the ineffectiveness and pedestrian incompetence of his superiors with their fixation on a government-led model of development which achieved little other than providing a gravy train for British expats with a vested interest in perpetuating the system. He eventually left his fast-track civil service career and returned to the UK to enter the London Business School MBA programme, after which he set up his own strategic and marketing consultancy. This prospered until he was stricken with a virus which laid him low for several months and wiped out his savings. By the time his health was finally restored his finances were in tatters and his wife was pregnant with their second child so in desperation he took the first job offer he could find, that of Development Economist in TCI. This was an ODA-sponsored role which would have reported to him a decade earlier when he was at the BDDC in Barbados and a job for which he was by then considerably over-qualified.

At a party given for him shortly after his arrival in March 1990 he was told 'not to try too hard, to bank (his) foreign service allowance and to serve (his) 'sentence' out without 'making waves'. Furious and despondent he was taken on a tour of the islands by his assistant Neville Adams and recently wrote the following description for me, to illustrate his awakening to the potential of the islands:

'For this, thanks to Neville Adams, who had chartered a Cessna for my second week.'

'Already depressed at what on earth I could do with Grand Turk, our first stop was South Caicos. My mood did not improve, even though the District Commissioner was charming. A hop over to Middle Caicos and I started feeling a bit better. Then north; a bit more life, some lovely beaches all along the Middle and North Coasts (Neville and the pilot were very accommodating in letting me explore every last cove)'

'Further west the Cays, then Leeward and Grace Bay. By the time we landed at Provo Airport, I was seriously excited. Then Turtle Cove, the Erebus Inn and Alfred's Place for the night. By the time I had met leading business people the next day, including Marc Redt in a working office in the middle of a half-completed hotel and a palpable air of energy and excitement, I knew there were huge possibilities. What would Barbados give for a couple of miles of this virgin beach within little more than an hour from Miami? The next day's trip to Leeward, Pine Cay and Parrot Cay were merely the icing on the cake. Having lived a stone's throw from Sandy Lane Hotel in Barbados for 3 years, I knew opportunity when I saw it.'

He knew from his earlier work for ODA that the same old approach, to appoint one of the large mainstream consultants to produce, at considerable cost, an economic development plan lacking any effective strategy for implementation but with several recommendations for expensive follow-up consultancy work, would achieve little other than helping the ODA spend its very substantial aid budget. What was needed was to re-focus government strategy towards the creation of private sector jobs which would lead to increases in government revenues and private savings and a decrease in the financial dependence on the UK. With great difficulty he persuaded a reluctant ODA to commission a wide-ranging strategic review of the economy, the first ever carried out in a British Dependent Territory.

Richard had considerable experience of working with consultants but had never come across Mokoro and was surprised when they were appointed. However he was encouraged to see that the team leader was to be Christopher Joubert who had been on the same course at the London Business School where he had supplemented his very extensive development experience with knowledge of the operations of the private sector. Richard insisted that Christopher visit the islands before the assignment began, took him on the same trip he had been taken on a few months earlier and managed to impart some of his enthusiasm for the great potential which the British administrators, who struggled to see beyond the difficulties of administering a reluctant colony, appeared unable to grasp.

My own journey through life from the outer suburbs of Surrey in early 1941 to this small tropical island in late 1990 had been interesting, erratic and unpredictable. Failure to get to Oxbridge led to a career in accountancy and that, combined with marriage to a Dane took me to Copenhagen for a couple of years, at the end of which we moved to Nairobi where I eventually left the accountancy profession and became involved in tourism and construction. The Kenya of immediate post-independence had a very enabling government which worked with the private sector to drive growth. After nine fascinating years the educational needs of my daughters brought us back to the UK where I established a consultancy looking after the financial affairs of British expatriates, mostly in the Arabian Gulf. I was eventually head-hunted by the Bahrain-based investment bank, giving me four years of extremely remunerative if rather unrewarding employment which came to such an abrupt end. By the time I arrived in TCI I had a diverse set of skills acquired during a varied career in accounting, financial services and tourism as well as the ability to deal with sudden reversals, the slings and arrows of outrageous fortune.

There were two other key people, both lawyers, whose very different personalities were factors in bringing about change. The Governor at the time, Michael Bradley, who had previously been Attorney General of the Cayman Islands, appeared to see his function mainly as a communications channel between Grand Turk and Whitehall and although he was not going to be proactive in shifting TCI out of its apparent lethargy, neither was he going to try to impede attempts to do so; and the acting attorney general, Lisa Agard who, unusually for many in that role, used her office to try to overcome obstacles to progress, rather than create them.

4. THE MOKORO STRATEGIC REVIEW

WHEN I HEARD THAT MOKORO'S proposal to carry out the strategic review of TCI had been accepted, with me on the team, I went to the local Library in my then home town of Farnham to find out what I could about the small island nation. As a schoolboy I had collected stamps so I knew the name of the islands but I had no idea where they were; they were simply one of many exotic-sounding and faraway tropical islands, Turks and Caicos, Cocos Keeling, Solomon and many others, small red specks on the map of the world, which issued colourful stamps all carrying the head of the British sovereign. The library enabled me to place them geographically and some of the entries suggested I was going somewhere very different to any country I had visited before. I had been used to the vibrant communities of Copenhagen, Nairobi and Bahrain: one of the four restaurants on Grand Turk thought worthy of a mention was Peanut's Conch Shack, which boasted two tables with a maximum capacity of eight and the only hotel listed on Middle Caicos, population 450, was Taylors Guest House with two rooms.

After Mokoro was appointed the BDDC insisted that as I had no experience of the Caribbean I spend a few days each in the Cayman Islands and Miami to get to know a little of the region and update my knowledge of tourism and offshore financial services. Life is strange: from being at an all-time low I was told to spend an extra week on what for many would be considered the trip of a lifetime.

Grand Cayman was more or less what I had expected, a handful of high-end hotels and a few more like the one in which I stayed, the clientele of which were predominantly sports divers: a slightly ramshackle building sitting on a low coral bluff with no beach but direct access to deep water from a wooden jetty built out over the rocks. Sitting in the bar with a cold beer at the end of the day, watching the sun setting over a calm tropical sea, hoping to see the elusive 'green flash' as the sun sank below the horizon, reminded me how much I love a warm climate. I realised what a battering I had taken during the previous months: this was the start of my healing. Twice each day I swam in the beautiful Caribbean, in the mornings out round the dive boats for exercise and in the late afternoon with mask and snorkel, drifting over the coral, unwinding at the end of the day, putting the shattering experiences at the turn of the year into perspective. I had my health and my family and was earning a modest amount, enough to see us through a few months. It was the start of the next phase of my life, one that was to take me to some beautiful places and introduce me to some extraordinary people.

During the days I did what I was sent to the island to do, meeting with lawyers, bankers and others engaged in the secretive world of offshore financial services, an industry in which the Cayman Islands were, and remain, a leading participant. Turks and Caicos was perhaps 15 years behind in this area and, as I was to find out, also in tourism. I met with a couple of people involved in hospitality and began to understand the significant benefits to a small island nation of a well-thought-out tourism policy and the dangers posed by unstructured development.

The Cayman Islands tourism industry caters largely for wealthy individual tourists staying in upmarket hotels and condominiums; other Caribbean nations had gone for the mass market, attracting far larger numbers of visitors but with the profits going almost entirely to the foreign hotel owners and tour operators. I also experienced for the first time the impact of cruise liners. While I was there several visited each day, anchored offshore, disgorged several thousand visitors who wandered vaguely round the shops, bought some typical tourist merchandise, perhaps had a drink then returned to the safety of the ship: that was Grand Cayman, they had been there, done that and had indeed in many cases bought the tee shirt. Grand Cayman was pleased to see them go, having gained little from their visit apart from a few dollars per head arrivals tax. Cruises are a huge component of Caribbean tourism but what little benefit they bring doesn't begin to offset the environmental damage they do.

On the last morning before leaving the island I had a final snorkel just outside town, drifting some ten feet above an unspectacular fairly monochrome coral reef, laid out almost in a grid looking for all the world like an American city viewed from above with deep chasms for the streets. It was teeming with fish, smallish ones on top but every now and then something larger moving deep down. A barracuda, my first, came purposefully up to have a look at me. It was only a baby, less than two feet long, but the fiercest looking fish I have ever seen. Remembering an episode from one of the early James Bond books I kept a careful eye on him in case he fancied any of my appendages. I returned to the hotel, checked out and headed to the airport. I had enjoyed my first visit to a Caribbean island, not one to fall in love with, but with a well-educated, confident and likeable mixed-race population where colour did not appear to be an issue, a thriving tourism industry and a professional community with connections in all the major centres of international finance. I headed to Miami to see what more I could glean in a brief couple of days.

My first impressions were coloured by the chaos of the immigration control at the airport. Inter-island Caribbean air travel is generally not well organised and it is usually simpler when going from one island to another to travel via Miami, which has become the regional hub. There are regular flights to all the main islands and Central American nations, at the time operated mostly by Pan Am and American Airlines. The layout of the airport, with no connection between its multiple terminals before immigration, did not generally allow for transit so it was necessary for all arriving passengers to clear immigration even if they were not remaining in the US. With strict immigration laws the seemingly endless flow of people arriving from countries where organised crime thrives on the South American drug trade resulted in regular people jams: queues of two or three hours were not unusual.

While in Miami I had a pre-arranged meeting with an organisation which styled itself 'The Turks and Caicos Islands Tourist Office' run by a mildly eccentric lady with origins in the Dominican Republic, Tina. I found out that Tina, with her husband Kit, once a sergeant in the US navy stationed on Grand Turk, had built one of the few hotels on Grand Turk, the Kittina. So that I could get a feel for TCI's tourism industry I asked Tina what the occupancy rate of their hotel was. 'How do you mean, occupancy rate?' she replied. I realised that the industry, such as it was, was hardly in the hands of professionals. A couple of years earlier Kit and Tina had been given a soft loan to fund the building of an extension to their hotel, a modern block of 20 or so bedrooms on the beach, ahead of a visit to the Island by Princess Alexandra in 1988; I found out later that they somehow never got round to servicing the loan, retaining in the US most of the revenue generated by the hotel. Some years later the hotel went into liquidation, the loan still unpaid, and was reborn as The Osprey Beach. The last time I saw Tina she was living in some comfort in Coral Gables, just south of Miami.

Before going on to the Turks and Caicos I made a short visit to Barbados to meet the people at the British Development Division to whom we would be reporting. The island is beautiful, the buildings in town old and dilapidated but with a certain charm. It was an interesting history lesson: walking the back-streets of the capital Bridgetown I came across the original synagogue, one of the earliest in the New World dating from 1654. I had no idea that, at the time Oliver Cromwell was consolidating his power base in England a Sephardic Jewish community was establishing itself in Barbados. They were led by refugees from Portuguese persecution in Brazil where they had been influential in the development of sugar plantations: bringing their skills to Barbados they were largely responsible for creating the industry which became an important source of England's wealth, the white gold of sugar effectively replacing the real stuff looted from the Spaniards by generations of English pirates.

I enjoyed the relaxed friendliness of the people, everyone happy to stop and talk. I was to experience this laid-back approach to life years later when I was team leader on a project to advise the Barbados government on the modernisation of their financial services industry. We were reporting to the Minister of Finance and in my first meeting with him I explained in some detail how we planned to carry out the assignment; he interrupted my slightly tiggerish enthusiastic flow with 'Yeah, man, but take some time to smell da roses'. Bajans are people I came to enjoy working with.

While there I made a goodwill visit to the British

High Commission and experienced one of those small coincidences which always remind me of how interconnected we are: while waiting in reception I was flipping through the visitors' book and saw that the third name on the first page, entered a few years earlier, was that of a good friend from Farnham with whom I'd recently had lunch.

After this week or so of enjoyable information-gathering, having superficially updated my knowledge of tourism I finally headed for the islands which were to play such a significant part in my life for the following few years.

* * *

Twice a week the Pan Am flight from Miami lands at Grand Turk International Airport, the only international commercial flight to do so. The airport, grandly named, is tiny, little more than a runway which straddles the island and a ramshackle structure to shelter the passengers during the longish wait for baggage, taken off the plane one item at a time. It is piled onto a pickup and trailer and driven at high speed to the modest terminal building; several cases invariably fall off en-route and have to be retrieved. Each piece is passed over a counter by hand to be claimed by its owner. The arrivals hall is open to the breezes, just as well as air-conditioning is non-existent. There are a handful of baggage carts and one porter, friendly and unfailingly cheerful.

Outside is leisurely chaos, a few taxis jostling for position, a small crowd of people meeting friends and relatives returning from Miami and others with nothing else to do but swap gossip, and where better to do that than at the airport? Most arrivals are local residents, burdened with cold-boxes and packing cases, trophies from shopping expeditions to Miami, goods unobtainable in the island's few shops. The taxis are directed by Ernie, an ex-minister who fell from grace after the Blom Cooper report, one of those deemed unfit to hold public office. He struts around purposefully, talking into a chunky walkie-talkie and for a few minutes twice a week imagines himself once again in a position of authority: he has no effect on the movements of the traffic. Peanuts Butterfield, a short, stout, elderly and myopic lady of Bermudan extraction sells drinks and sweets from a coldbox. Given half a chance she will tell you of her close friendship with the British Royal family, having been present on the island when Prince Philip and Prince Charles visited years ago, and more recently having introduced herself to Princess Alexandra.

After 20 minutes the aging Pan Am 727 which has briefly dwarfed the humble airport building fires up its engines and takes to the skies to return to the comparative sophistication of Miami, the small crowd disperses and Grand Turk International Airport, this brief moment of excitement over, returns to its sleepy self.

* * *

I took a taxi from the airport to the Kittina Hotel, was shown up to my beachfront room on the first floor, stood on the balcony looking out over the pale golden beach to the flat summer-calm turquoise water and the cloudless sky and for the first time in many months felt completely at peace. Life sometimes does that, knocks you down when you least expect it then gently lifts you up and says 'there, there, I didn't mean it, see, I've opened a new door'.

That evening I met the others from the Mokoro team: Christopher, the Team Leader, a dry and pedantic South-African-born economist with, as I soon found out, a brilliant analytical mind; Martin, a land-use specialist with many years of consulting in Africa, tall, slightly shaggy, a man who only ever wore Rohan trousers and plaid shirts and somehow should, but didn't, smell of pipe tobacco; Tony, a fisheries expert who spent his life in and around tropical seas from St Helena to Vanuatu; Jennifer, formidable and fun, an economist who had been working in Tanzania when I first met her a decade earlier and who remains a good friend; Phil, a sociologist whose rural Welsh background made him well suited to understanding the attitudes of comparatively isolated small-island communities; Ian, an engineer experienced in the design and construction of small-community infrastructure, and me. The contrast with my colleagues in investment banking could not have been more stark; their job had been to make extremely rich people even richer and to accumulate their own not-insignificant wealth along the way; the Mokoro team was charged with re-inventing the economy of a small nation for the benefit of all its people, a task which I hoped would be rather more fulfilling. It would certainly be more challenging.

As a team we were supported by the economics section of the finance office, Richard who had commissioned the study, his feisty, efficient and loyal secretary Mavis and Neville, his assistant and general fixer. Our office was at South Base, abandoned by the US military a decade or so earlier and now home to much of the civil service; we were allocated a large room in the staff training unit, part of the Chief Secretary's office. The Base sits on a small rocky promontory with the sea on three sides. It was subject to the occasional Atlantic storm and showed distinct signs of age but its standard units of two offices with a bathroom in between were quite functional. There were three parallel rows of these offices: the Attorney General and Department of Lands to the west, the Chief Secretary who is responsible for the smooth running of the civil service, and Education in the middle and Finance in the east. This arrangement meant that most of those involved in the day-to-day running of the islands were within a minute or so's walk of each other; as we soon found out it did not necessarily mean they were on speaking terms.

There is no public transport on Grand Turk and Mokoro, ever frugal, had a minimal budget for local travel, so to avoid the expense of taxis a modest amount was available for the purchase of a second-hand vehicle; Neville had found us, for a few hundred dollars, a little red Ford Fiesta, a name which suited the slightly carnival atmosphere never far away on Caribbean islands. Generally only two or three of us were in the car at the same time but on rare occasions we all needed to travel together, seven of us in a two-door four seater. I recall us all crowding in and going to a meeting at the Governor's office, emerging at our destination like some crumpled tropical Keystone Cops; it is hard, working in such circumstances, to avoid the occasional element of slapstick. Somehow it seemed natural given the superficially relaxed Mokoro approach; I cannot help but think that any of the mainstream firms of consultants would have found a more elegant, and considerably more expensive, transport solution.

Each of us had our own area of expertise and the strategy was to spend some three weeks interviewing as many as possible of the influencers in the islands, the movers and shakers from all walks of life, in order to build up a composite picture of the islands' life as it was and as they would want it to be, what the islanders themselves wanted for their small and still very dependent nation. We gave as much weight to the views of fishermen and school teachers as to those of the politicians. Looking back we probably gave more weight to members of the general public than to those in power. The pool of information we gained during those three weeks would allow us to model what the society could become if the appropriate resources were made available (a couple of the team were economists and there is little that economists like better than modelling). We would then hold a two-day workshop where we could feed our findings back so that the residents, both native and expatriate, would understand the consequences of their wishes, with elements of 'be careful what you wish for'.

My brief was to study the tourism and financial services sectors and recommend a strategy for their development. The third leg of the productive economy was fishing, which was Tony's field – I knew little about the breeding habits of conch and lobster. It is an interesting reflection on the thinking of the Overseas Development Authority who were funding the study that of a team of seven charged with creating a dynamic strategy for growth only two were to study that which actually generates the income, the other five looking into government finances, the sociological impact of growth and such like. There is, in the mindset of many in the public sector, an assumption that wealth somehow creates itself and with it the attitude that the regulation and channelling of wealth is more important than its creation.

Meeting new people is for me one of life's great pleasures so to be paid to spend time on some tropical islands and meet as many as possible of its inhabitants suited me well. For logistical reasons most of my time at the start of the assignment was on Grand Turk, which was still home to much of the small financial services industry, the lawyers, accountants and corporate management firms. They were an interesting collection. The doyen of the industry was an Irishman who had been sent out in the mid '70s as magistrate and used to travel round the islands dispensing justice from the back of a donkey. There were two brothers from New Zealand, one a lawyer, the other an accountant, who had drifted in on their travels some years earlier and stayed on; a small handful of mainly public-school-educated Englishmen, black sheep making a living away from their establishment families; a motley collection of lawyers from North America and the Caribbean and a few Turks Islanders who had managed to get themselves a professional education. As I got to know them I began to understand why TCI lagged behind the Cayman Islands as a centre for offshore financial services. During my own career I had gained some experience of such activities, having set up my first offshore company in the Cayman Islands nearly 20 years earlier. (I had used the Cayman Islands because an accountant colleague from Nairobi had moved there and we used to correspond. He told me that on the small island of Cayman Brac there were only two roads and only two cars using them: late one New Year's Eve they collided. It sounded like the sort of place to which I could relate.) I quickly realised that, despite the ambitions of the professional community, the financial services industry, while giving a small number of islanders the opportunity to become professionally qualified and creating a limited number of alternative employment opportunities, would always be secondary to tourism as the prime driver of the economy.

As our work progressed we came to realise that almost everyone knew everyone else. Word of our assignment spread very rapidly and we were met mostly with 'Oh yes, just another group of overpaid British consultants going through the motions who will produce one more report on these over-studied islands, to sit and gather dust in ODA's offices.' This was understandable, given how many ineffectual and unimaginative reports on how to develop TCI had been written in the past. I was new to such work but the others had considerable experience and were unconcerned by this reaction. Mokoro had an exceptional track record of bringing about change; given the right strategic direction TCI was very obviously poised for growth and such growth, if properly managed, could be channelled to benefit the whole nation.

* * *

Grand Turk had a total of some 40 hotel rooms, half in the Kittina, the others in a couple of old merchants' houses, The Saltraker and The Turks Head, which had been converted into small but comfortable hotels, and a handful of small guest houses. The Turks Head was at the time closed for renovation and remained closed for some years. The majority of visitors to Grand Turk were there on Government business, most of the rest for the diving, among the finest in the Caribbean. On the west side of the island a few hundred yards out from the beach there is a sheer two thousand metre wall, home to beautiful soft corals and less beautiful but equally fascinating moray eels and vertical hunting grounds for eagle rays and an occasional visiting manta; to the east are large areas of sea grass studded with coral heads, a rich nursery for the turtles which hatch every year on the deserted beach and home to graceful and balletic sting rays. This varied marine life attracts a small number of dedicated divers prepared to forego the sybaritic delights of better-known destinations. Visiting divers were catered for at the time by two small but well run operations, Blue Water Divers set up by Mitch, an American singer/songwriter and hugely experienced diving instructor who'd drifted in ten years earlier, and Sea Eye Diving belonging to Cecil, the first Turks Islander to qualify as a divemaster. In addition to his diving Mitch provided the musical entertainment at the

Saltraker two evenings a week.

There was a small handful of restaurants catering to visitors and local residents. At one end of the gastronomic spectrum, selling nothing but conch fritters with spicy sauce, was Peanuts' Conch Shack with its two tables seating 8 people, at the other was X's, slightly inland facing the large salina, run by Xavier, an artistic, alcoholic and heavy-smoking Frenchman. X's wife and mistress had recently both left him to form their own partnership, personal as well as professional, and set up a competing restaurant a few yards away at the top of the beach. Both served excellent French food.

The restaurant at the Saltraker was a rambling informal tree-studded courtyard with mis-matched furniture scattered around the central horseshoe-shaped bar. Off to one side there was a corrugated iron kitchen shack from which slightly alarming smoke often oozed but from where good food always emerged. The Saltraker, owned, in one of life's small coincidences, by a friend of my brother-in-law in Ascot, was efficiently managed by Jenny, whose soon-to-be-ex husband Chris spent most of his time at the bar, but the restaurant was the domain of Elaine. Elaine was a big woman, tall, broad, statuesque and feisty with a large face and large features and a large heart. She managed a small team including Anna Mae, also large but calmer and slower, sweet and gentle: Anna Mae was, much later, to give me lessons in dancing, Island style.

Good food was not a feature of the decidedly uninviting restaurant at the Kittina, where Kit and Tina's haphazard management style was partly compensated for by the efficient Ivy, in many ways the complete opposite to Elaine. Ivy was also tall but thin as a reed, kind and sociable but in all the years I was to know her I cannot once recall her smiling.

That was the hospitality industry on Grand Turk in

1990. Looking back it has hardly developed in the 30 years that have passed, although there have been some changes for the better. Jenny, now happily remarried, eventually bought the Kittina out of receivership, Kit and Tina having given up any pretence of intending to repay their loans, and it has been completely renovated and reborn as the Osprey Beach Hotel. A couple of smaller inland hotels have opened, and that is pretty much the sum total of three decades of tourism development on Grand Turk.

After a couple of weeks on Grand Turk I flew over to Providenciales, 'Provo'. Inter-island travel was delightfully informal. There were more or less regular flights by Turks and Caicos National Airline, which struggled to live up to its impressive name. When the sales lady handed me my first ticket I looked at the card envelope in which it was presented and was not filled with confidence: I immediately spotted a simple typographical error – Grand Turk appeared on the small stylised route map as 'Grand Truk'. Most people preferred to take pot luck with one of the aging six-seater Piper Cherokees which a handful of amateur pilots flew back and forth between Grand Turk and Provo, charging $50 per seat for the 60 mile journey, taking off when they had enough passengers to make the flight worthwhile. Occasionally one of them failed to complete the journey in the conventional way but fatalities were rare – there are many things more dangerous than landing a light plane on a flat sea. I came to love it as a relaxed way of travel. The joy of have a 10 minute walk to the airport to get there 5 minutes before take-off time, to know the pilot (and indeed most of the other passengers and the people working at the airport) and then to fly a few hundred feet above a chain of tropical islands was infinitely nicer than flying with Ryanair from Stansted Airport.

On Provo I stayed at the only modern hotel on the

island, the newly opened Ramada, and spent a few days meeting as many as possible of the participants in the loosely-defined tourism industry. I met with ambitious would-be hotel developers, I sat in on meetings of the taxi drivers association, I had a few beers with fishermen and dropped in on the couple of dive shops. I discovered that 'consultancy' like this was right up my street. In the most enjoyable way I gradually built up a picture of the existing capabilities and future potential of the islands.

Provo, with its miles of white sand beaches, was more obviously attractive to tourists. Club Med had built their trade-mark units of basic accommodation with large central facilities and young North Americans came in their droves to enjoy casual romance in a tropical setting. Their business model is based on keeping its visitors within the compound and all of them were told in the welcoming talk that it was dangerous to leave the Club compound as crime was rife on the outside. At that time this was offensive nonsense: crime was almost non-existent. Provo had a population of some 5000 and everyone seemed not only to know everyone else but also what they were each up to. While Club Med itself did little for the economy of the islands, being built by imported labour with imported materials and staffed with imported people, as part of the deal which HMG made with them five years earlier the airport had been built, the crucial first building block for a viable industry. For the first time Providenciales had scheduled international flights, three a week from Miami. In addition to the Ramada, constructed with support from the local government, there was only one other hotel of any size, the Island Princess which had been built extremely cheaply a few years earlier by an American entrepreneur; it would not have met any normal safety standards. There was also one major half-completed resort hotel, supposedly to be part of the Sheraton chain but it had a complex ownership structure and inadequate funding and its development had stalled.

Attracted by the airport and pristine beaches a few developers had started to build very much better facilities, mainly up-market condominiums which are the ideal foundation for an inclusive tourism industry. They are used mostly by the owners and their friends who tend to spend on local services, restaurants, shops, boats, taxis and hire cars, ensuring that the community in general benefits from their visits. Among the condominium developers two stood out, Ron Ohliger and Klaus Kreis. Ron, from the US, had constructed the first couple of blocks of the excellent Ocean Club; he spent much of his time there and took a very personal interest. Klaus, from a wealthy family of Swiss industrialists, had just started the building of Grace Bay Club to an even higher standard. Eventually I got to know them both fairly well. A couple of personal anecdotes: once when I was staying at Ocean Club where Ron used to let me have a small room at the back at nominal cost I accidentally locked myself out. I was told by the staff that he had the only master key but had gone out to dinner at the local Tex Mex restaurant, so I called and he immediately drove back and let me in, not the sort of service you get at a chain hotel; and a couple of years later I was having dinner with Klaus at Grace Bay when the wind got up and he noticed I was cold; I accepted his offer of the loan of a Pringle sweater, which turned out to have a large hole in one elbow. Given that Klaus is a very wealthy man I found that somehow rather touching.

It was obvious to any visitor that unlike that of Grand Turk, Provo's tourism industry was poised for growth and that this would be driven largely by wealthy expatriates who felt no allegiance to the government on Grand Turk, to the obvious annoyance of most of the local ministers. Development was going to continue in spite of the best efforts of Grand Turk and the British government to rein it in. Grand Turk, unlike Provo, was largely sheltered from financial reality by British funding; there were enough government jobs to go round so why encourage development which would only complicate life?

The distance between these two main islands, geographical as well as philosophical, was both a strength and a weakness. The strength was in the comparative absence of government interference on Provo. Grand Turk, home to most of the hidebound civil service, was both jealous and nervous of the increasingly rapid development on Provo. Like civil services everywhere it lacked real-life business experience, leading to problems in distinguishing between genuine investors, dreamers and crooks so it was probably fair to say that the less direct involvement it had, the better for the industry.

The weakness was a lack of commitment by the government to actively and effectively promote the industry or to attempt to understand or address the major constraints to growth. Some years earlier the Tourism Office had been set up but it was inadequately staffed and had neither an office nor representation on Provo. It was indicative of the attitude of government that the office they reluctantly set up to promote tourism was not on Provo, the island which had begun to attract tourists but on Grand Turk which has little to offer. The Tourism Office manager spent most of the limited budget on shopping trips to Miami and New York and as she was the mistress of the Chief Minister, who was also Minister for Tourism, nothing was done to stop her.

While Tony and I were exploring the potential for growth in the productive sectors of the economy the rest of the team were considering the infrastructure, both physical and administrative, which would be required to support such growth and the implications it had for the structure and life of the community. The sociological impact would be considerable; we had discussed at length the bias held by Turks Islanders against Haitians; most of the islanders we spoke to didn't want Haitians coming to live in TCI, except of course for 'their' Haitians who did menial work for them. As an example, only Turks Islanders could buy fishing licences but few of the fishermen were prepared to do the hard work of diving for conch. Tony's description of fishing methods neatly summed this up: 'They drive their high-powered boat as fast as possible out to the fishing grounds, lob their Haitian over the side and settle back with a beer.' With the peculiar prejudice between different sectors of the black community which I've come across in other places the Chief Minister had said to me 'you Brits bring in black people to work on the London underground, why shouldn't we bring in Haitians to do our dirty work?' The need for growth in immigration implicit in our projections and the impact it would have on this small and slightly xenophobic island had to be handled diplomatically.

Drawing together all our findings we held a workshop at the Ramada Hotel, the first use of its full conference facilities, to which we invited two hundred of the most important people in the islands. Not 'important' as in high up the social scale, but a cross section of those who had influence and opinions on where the Islands should go. They say that there are three types of people: those who make things happen, those who let things happen and those who wonder what happened. This audience was drawn mainly from the first category and ranged from the ministers to taxi drivers and fishermen, most of whom I had met during the preceding few weeks. The event ran for two-days and the entire proceedings were broadcast live on Radio Turks and Caicos.

The local Government ministers occupied the front

row, the Chief Minister in the centre. He was a Caribbean politician straight out of central casting and, as I was to find out much later when he was my boss and his mistress my subordinate, a thoroughly unpleasant man. Nothing in his training had equipped him to run a country, even a very small one, and he covered that up by wearing flashy suits and dark glasses. For the workshop he was wearing a particularly garish creation of mustard-yellow and lime-green checks. Around him were the other ministers including Wendell, slightly built and intelligent, recently returned from Aberystwyth University with a good degree, Lew, a charming, sociable laid back and moderately successful local entrepreneur, Big Louie, with a great mass of curly black hair and beard, shirt open to his waist, gold medallion perched on his substantial stomach, a children's picture-book image of a pirate, and a couple of others. The phrase 'motley crew' came to mind. Off to the side of the room, close to the front, were two brothers, Washington and Michael Misick, leading members of the opposition, very different characters but both to become Chief Minister in subsequent years.

It was apparent to us that with the right application of resources, both financial and managerial, the possibilities for growth were considerable, and in our discussions with Turks Islanders almost all had expressed the desire to see high growth in the economy, on the quite natural assumption that it would bring corresponding growth in individual incomes. We needed to convey the message that maximum growth for its own sake was not necessarily in the country's best interests but if our report was to be accepted and implemented the major decisions had to be seen to have been taken by the people as a whole.

On the first day Christopher presented three different scenarios, low, medium and high growth, and explained the effect of each on society, graphically shown on a screen behind us as a 3 x 3 matrix with growth on one axis, the projected population on the other and in each box a brief description of the probable impact on society. We explained that high growth would require a substantial increase in immigration, with expatriates from Haiti and the Dominican Republic at one end of the social scale and from North America and Europe at the other, and this would have considerable sociological implications for what had been, up till then, a sleepy Caribbean backwater. It was very noticeable that the confident smiles were replaced by looks of concern. Some of the more vocal and less thoughtful, the Chief Minister among them, argued, almost demanded, that we should be proposing maximum growth with no population increase; Christopher struggled to restrain himself but eventually got the message across.

Having spent three weeks out and about in the wider community I had probably met more of the audience members than my colleagues so I was chosen to chair the second day; it was stimulating, challenging and exhausting. It was important to encourage wide participation from the audience so that the people and not just the politicians would buy in to the conclusions drawn from the workshop. There were contributions from Ernie the taxi-driving ex-minister, from Chuck, six foot six ex US submarine commander now running the world's only conch farm, and from Smoky who ran a notorious bar on the beach; there was a long and rambling complaint from a lady with obvious mental health issues who would only relinquish the microphone when I instructed someone to pull the plug; and of course I discovered that as with political meetings the world over many of the audience saw it as a platform to further their own causes. My job as Chair, in addition to allowing the ordinary people to have their say was to try to give equal weighting to each political group. I had learnt as I got to know the islanders that they hold their political allegiances very strongly and some of them had made a point of telling me which party they supported very early in our conversations. The Chief Minister with his regulation impenetrable dark glasses and yellow and green suit, sitting right in front of me, made very political points attacking both the opposition party and the British policy towards its overseas territories. As far as possible I allowed Washington Misick as leader of the opposition, rather more conservatively dressed, a legacy of his accountancy background, equal time to talk about his vision for the islands; I noted that he took a positive forward view of the possibilities whereas the Chief Minister was backward looking and negative. After Washington had made a long and rambling political statement his younger brother Michael, still in his mid-twenties and, as I later found out, with the fierce ambition of a youngest child who had not managed to attain the professional qualifications of some of his siblings, got to his feet to speak: time was running out and as politely as I could I stopped him with 'perhaps that's enough from the Misicks, can we hear from someone else?' He glowered but sat down.

Towards the end of a very long day I was taking written questions passed up from the floor and handed to me by my colleague Jennifer. I unfolded one slip and read, 'You must get the name of his tailor!' Trying to keep a straight face I rapidly moved on to a real question. As I was wrapping up what had to my surprise been a very productive session I asked for one last question. 'I gotta question,' growled Big Louie. 'You wanna job?'

The meeting closed and with my Mokoro colleagues I headed for the bar for a well-earned beer. I was followed by the Misicks and as I turned to speak to them Mike, who I learned later is at heart a thug, tried to take a swing at me but was restrained by his older brother. I got to know them both very well in the following years. They became very different Chief Ministers, Washington creating the platform for the development of the Islands, Mike utterly venal and with his corruption pretty much destroying what had become a vibrant economy.

As an aside, the day after the workshop Big Louie invited me to his office as he wanted some advice on a property development in which he was involved. As he produced the relevant plans I saw that he took time working out which way up they should be and I realised that he was at best only semi-literate. I found out later that he had a history of arson, being implicated in the burning down in the mid-1980s of one of Grand Turk's historic nineteenth century buildings; a year or so later his car spontaneously caught fire outside the parliament building while he was inside as a member of the Legislative Assembly, the source of the fire being traced to the large amount of cannabis stashed in the boot, of which he claimed no knowledge. Politics in the Caribbean may not be as sophisticated as it is in Europe but in its own way it is just as interesting.

The outcome of the workshop was that while most people still claimed to want maximum growth they would be happy with less if it meant that jobs and opportunities would still be created and the main beneficiaries would be Turks Islanders. We spent the next three weeks feeding all that back into our projections and drafting our reports. There was of course the occasional disagreement but nothing of substance. Christopher, of South African origin, pedantic and precise, and Jennifer, Australian, witty and outgoing, were not, metaphorically, natural bed-fellows. I recall an instance when Jen had used the word 'optimistic'. 'The correct word, Jennifer, is sanguine'. 'No' says Jen, 'I mean optimistic'. 'We will stick to 'sanguine', Jennifer'.

Christopher, as team leader, had the ultimate say so there was no further discussion. He did not, I think, consider it any sort of a victory, pedantic he might be but never petty. It was simply the need to use absolutely the best and most suitable words. I was fortunate enough to once hear Seamus Heaney talking about poetry, which he described as being 'the best words in the best order'. Christopher, who would be the first to accept that he is not a wordsmith in the class of Heaney, had the same attitude to words when writing his reports. And perhaps Australians are optimistic where South Africans are sanguine. During the report-writing period Richard, ever enthusiastic, continued to feed in ideas and insights. Christopher, showing signs of stress, he told him in a fairly forceful manner, 'Richard, I cannot add any more. We have a deadline, you know. I must re-emphasise what you already know; the drawbridge has already been raised.'

Back in England we each completed our drafting and Christopher melded the various contributions into a cohesive report, smoothing our individual styles into a uniform whole, with our conclusions and recommendations which, if they were acted upon, would set the country on a path to steady growth with minimal societal disruption. He and I returned to TCI in late January and spent a week presenting our report to the Executive Council which comprised the local government ministers, the Chief Secretary, the Attorney General and the Governor who chairs it. At the end of our presentation and the subsequent discussions I wondered whether or not we had got any of our messages across. We had developed and recommended a clear strategy for private-sector-led development to take the islands away from dependence on UK aid and government jobs but it was obvious that the management of the islands needed a complete shake-up and personalities and egos stood in the way. Ours was simply the latest in a long line of 'studies' which the Council assumed would, like all the others, soon lie forgotten, gathering dust on the ODA's shelves. The Governor asked why we thought our report would have more effect than its predecessors; Christopher, as ever choosing his words with extreme care, replied 'Oh Governor, I do hope you are not inciting me to vanity!'

As it happened The Mokoro Report was officially adopted as a strategic plan for the development of TCI, sold more copies, at $20 each, than any other Government publication before or since and was used as a blueprint for similar studies in other UK Overseas territories. I was invited back to set up a tourist board and be Director of Tourism and TCI went on to achieve the highest growth rate in the Caribbean for the following decade. Years later, looking back on his long career in overseas development Christopher remarked that the Turks and Caicos Strategic Review achieved more and led to more real and successful change than any other assignment that he ever worked on.

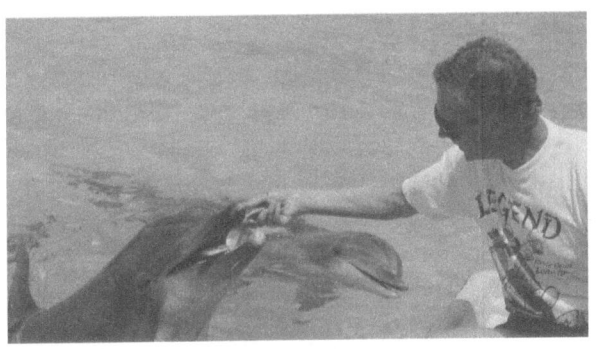

5. THE TOURIST BOARD

WITH THE ACCEPTANCE OF THE Mokoro report by the Executive Council I was given a short contract to turn the very inefficient Tourist Office into a fully-fledged Tourist Board, acting as interim Director of Tourism. My contract was for an initial period of three months extendible for another three, the first half to get the office running efficiently, the second to identify and recruit my successor.

A supervisory board had been appointed, drawn mainly from people involved in the tourism industry; it included Tina, the hotelier I had visited in Miami who appeared not to know what 'occupancy rate' meant and why it was quite important, Clifford, the owner of a small hotel on North Caicos who I got to know well and who, it was rumoured, had had some peripheral involvement in the drugs traffic of the 1980s, Josephine, the Assistant Permanent Secretary in the Chief Ministers Office, and a few others, mainly from the private sector.

I had visited the office in the course of the Mokoro study and had found it uninviting, chaotic and untidy, every surface covered with piles of papers gathering dust and a general air of lethargy and inefficiency. With only five incoming scheduled flights a week, all from Miami, two to Grand Turk and three to Provo, and most of the passengers residents of the islands the number of visitors was negligible, 50,000 annually according to the rather unreliable statistics, Half of these were for Club Med, which was of course a world apart and of which I'll write later, and many of the remainder were on government business. Very few were tourists who had made the positive decision to visit the Turks and Caicos Islands.

Before I returned to the islands I discussed with my wife the approach I would take, how I would shake them up from day one. 'Don't' she said. 'They've never been taught how to do their job and you'll only antagonise them'. She was of course right. On the first day I turned up and introduced myself to the staff. The office had been run by Norma, the Chief Tourism Officer who was to be my deputy, and two assistants, Pauline, a slow, gentle soul who carried an air of serenity with her, and Gracita, Sita, her polar opposite, slim, beautiful and energetic, her name and golden skin coming from her roots in the Dominican Republic which lay some ninety miles to the south. There was an office junior, Hyacinth, and a messenger, Talmadge, in his late teens, raised in the expatriate Turks Islander community in the neighbouring Bahamas. I introduced myself and was met by fairly open hostility from Norma and wariness from the others.

The office was in a mess. None of the basic equipment, essential for the efficient functioning of any office, was working properly. The computer, printer and telephone answering machine (vital, as there was an expensive 0800 number for potential visitors to call toll-free from the U.S.) didn't work at all and the photocopier was playing up. There were bags of letters waiting to be posted as there was no franking machine and no one had bothered to buy any stamps and the recording of visitor statistics was six months behind. These statistics are extracted from the arrival forms which all incoming tourists fill out at the airport, showing countries of origin and other information useful for marketing the Islands; on the many, many times I have gone through the chore of filling out immigration forms I imagined that they at least served some useful purpose in keeping track of visitors: in TCI they were simply offloaded to the tourist office where they gathered dust for a while before being tallied, totals entered on a spreadsheet, filed and forgotten. I began to wonder what I could achieve in my initial three months.

There was a strong temptation to get angry and force them to face up to the consequences of their obvious neglect but I heeded my wife's advice and chose instead to lead by example and be proactive in setting things right. I decided that the best initial use of my time was to at least get the office equipment functioning. While trying to work out what was wrong with the computer I saw Talmadge emptying a whole can of insect spray into the box of the then-ubiquitous 4" disks used for storing what little visitor data was extracted from the immigration forms. I asked him why; he replied 'de ants dey be nessin in deah' which I translated from his heavy Bahamian accent to mean 'there is an ants nest in there!' Sure enough all the expensively-gathered visitor data, essential for the properly targeted marketing of TCI as a tourist destination, had been destroyed by a nest of tiny ants and nobody seemed to care. I called the government IT department who sent someone to fix the computer, found a new box of disks and persuaded Pauline and Sita to begin entering the 6-month backlog of data – Norma obviously considered such work beneath her.

I made a cursory check of the answering machine and found it had no battery. 'Would it help if I bought one?' I asked Norma. 'Mebbe', was her sullen reply, so I walked to a nearby shop and did so. When I played back the recorded message I heard Norma's voice saying, 'you have reached the Turks and Caicos Tourist Office' in a flat and uninviting monotone which carried in it the unspoken subtext 'in spite of all our efforts'. I re-recorded it to sound rather more welcoming, hoping that my very English accent might be a plus for some American callers.

It had been an interesting first day, depressing to start with but improving with the realisation that the staff, used to the negativity of Norma and her counterparts in the ministry, responded well to a little positive action. I met Richard for a beer at the Saltraker where I had a quiet supper mulling over the challenges facing me before returning to the Kittina where I was staying until I could find a room to rent.

The next morning, in a more positive frame of mind I spent a little time with each of the staff, getting to know them and hopefully letting them get to know me. Mid-morning I walked the few yards to the office of the Chief Minister who was also Minister of Tourism, Oswald Skippings, universally known as Skip, him of the dark glasses and garish suits. I soon found out that for all his cunning he was not the brightest of people. I asked him what his vision for tourism in the islands was: 'We've got the greatest beaches in the world, and I want as many people as possible to enjoy them before they get ruined.' I enjoy a challenge but that told me I was going to have something of an uphill struggle.

A short walk from my office was the post office, housed in a nineteenth century whitewashed building on the seafront. It was one of the focal points of the community, staffed by ladies who enjoyed a gossip. There was, as with so much of the island's civil service, very little sense of urgency. Post came and went of course but the most profitable activity of the post office was the sale of the beautiful postage stamps which represented a significant source of income for the government. Every design, and there were several new issues each year, apparently had to be personally approved by the Queen as they carried her portrait. These stamps, the sale of which was out of all proportion to the volume of post leaving the islands, were the only reason why I, and many thousands of other young stamp collectors, had heard of The Turks and Caicos Islands. On my first visit to the post office shortly after starting at the Tourist Board I noticed that one of the ladies' chair had a broken leg and she was supporting it with a well-stuffed post bag. I suggested that she ask the maintenance department to find a replacement chair, which she did; the postbag was belatedly opened and the contents, including a fair number for the tourist board, were duly distributed, some weeks late.

* * *

After staying at The Kittina for a few days I found a delightful bed and breakfast less than a minute's walk from my new office, belonging to a retired couple, Doug and Angie. They had previously owned The Saltraker Hotel which they had converted from a lovely old 19th century salt-merchant's house sitting in a grove of casuarinas at the top of the beach, just north of the Kittina. Doug was a one-time high-flying Hollywood publicity agent who had decided to leave the rat race, live the dream and run a Caribbean hotel, Angie an ex schoolteacher originally from the UK. They were both divorced, met on Grand Turk and got together. So they didn't have to describe in detail the trials and tribulations, the excitement and setbacks of the development of The Saltraker a decade earlier they leant me a book, 'Don't Stop the Carnival' by Herman Wouk and told me it could have been based on their experiences. I recommend it as a delightful read. They were an ideal match, both physically and intellectually, tall, slim and attractive, each with a silver pony tail, living a quiet life doing worthwhile things in the community and staying well clear of anything political. They had a little shop selling ornaments which Doug made from sea-shells, and a house in Lincolnshire which they visited a couple of times a year. Angie told her British friends that she had achieved a lifetime ambition to become a seaside landlady.

Grand Turk at the time would not appeal to the average tourist; the facilities were decidedly limited and life was full of minor frustrations but it was a wonderful place in which to escape from everyday life. The 'door' to my upstairs room, accessed by an outside staircase open to the world, was a wire mesh screen which had no lock; inside I had my camera, videocam and a laptop but it was unthinkable that anyone on the island would steal anything. One evening Doug and Angie invited me to join them for dinner to meet a friend, one of their regular visitors, an American paediatrician from Louisville Kentucky, who had been coming to Grand Turk on vacation every year since 1974. I asked her if she ever went anywhere else: Long pause, then 'Ah cain't say as ah do!' The way she put it, in an accent I couldn't possibly imitate and with a voice that would cut through concrete, it made complete sense: she worked under great stress throughout the year and when she took a break she wanted complete relaxation and there was nowhere better for that than Grand Turk. I understood. Where else in the world would a taxi driver stop to offer a lift, and not charge because it was a hot day and I had looked tired, as happened to me a few days after I arrived? After I'd been on the island a month or so, long enough to be recognised, I went shopping at one of the two supermarkets, got to the checkout and found I hadn't enough cash. 'No problem, pay us next time.' I wouldn't like to try that in Sainsbury's.

I discovered that this trusting attitude wasn't a one-off. Years later I flew, with a small TCI-based airline, from Provo to Haiti for a weekend visit. When I checked in for the return flight I was told there was a departure tax of $50 and that credit cards were not accepted. I didn't have sufficient cash and asked the man operating the check-in what I could do. He immediately took $50 from his wallet, handed it to me and said 'pay it to Harold when you get back to Provo.' Harold was the owner of the airline, who I, along with almost everyone else on Provo, knew casually.

During my first few weeks at the Tourist Board there were times of considerable stress, battles with Norma and some of the civil servants and politicians, and Doug and Angie were a great support and source of encouragement. I would walk back from the office, discuss the fun and games of the day over a cup of tea (both were recovering alcoholics and didn't drink) then put on swimming shorts, take a mask and snorkel and cross the road to swim from the little triangle of sand below the sea wall. There were not many fish, the coral below having been killed off by two centuries of the comings and goings of salt merchants' boats but I had the occasional company of a juvenile barracuda or small turtle, sometimes a graceful eagle ray making an afternoon visit from outside the reef to see what the shallower waters had to offer. Refreshed, my mind once more at rest, I would retire upstairs to my veranda and relax with a book and a gin and tonic or rum punch as the sun went down over the sea separating us from South Caicos. The osprey would survey his kingdom from the telecommunications tower, occasionally a humpback whale would blow out a plume of spray as it made it's slow way back to New England from the breeding grounds on the Silver Banks some fifty miles south, and I found a level of peace which I hadn't known since I left East Africa 15 eventful years earlier.

I last saw Doug and Angie some 25 years later. They had moved to the small neighbouring island of Salt Cay with its community of fewer than 100 people; they spent a third of their time there, a third in Lincolnshire and a third at a house they had bought on the coast of Turkey. A delightful couple from whom I learnt much about life's priorities.

* * *

Early in my working life I had spent some exciting and fulfilling years in the heady atmosphere of immediate-post-independence Kenya where much of the population, regardless of race or nationality, was working together in an atmosphere of optimism to develop the country; an exception was the staff of the British High Commission who still had a distinctly negative colonial attitude. I found parallels in TCI: during the Mokoro study I had found that I didn't really relate to the small community of British Technical Co-operation Officers with their counterproductive negativity. I realised that if my very short assignment was to be effective and the tourist industry steered in a way that would benefit the islanders I had to get to know and understand, and in return be accepted by, the local community; being seen to socialise with the TCOs was a sure way of preventing that. I knew that during my short time on the island I would never be accepted as a local but I also knew from my time in Kenya that the relationship of an expat to the local community is very nuanced and that community soon picks up whose side you are on. I knew that I would have more impact and get more professional satisfaction by being on their side.

There were also personal considerations: I was beginning to accept that my marriage was no longer happy and that my work-related travels were an escape from the difficulties of home. During my years of living and working in other countries I had had much enjoyment from mixing with people outside the usual expatriate circles: I needed the comfort of being part of a community and for a time I found it on Grand Turk.

Having established myself in the office and got to know the staff I set out to find out what was being done to promote tourism. The efforts and the expenditure seemed to be concentrated on Norma's regular visits to tourism trade fairs in New York and an annual trip to the World Travel Market exhibition in London. She was usually accompanied by Josephine, chair of the Tourist Board, to whom she had reported before I arrived. There were PR agents in New York and London whose main functions seemed to be to organise Norma's trips, which centred more on shopping than tourism: I had made a point of meeting the London agent before coming out to the Islands and found she had serious alcohol problems; meetings with her were only productive if they took place in the morning.

To draw up a strategy for the development of the nascent tourism industry I needed to find out what both the natural environment and the built infrastructure had to offer. Providenciales and the Caicos Islands have beaches as fine as any I have seen, mile after mile of pure white sand fringed with palm trees and casuarinas and lapped by a gentle turquoise sea, the whole protected from the Atlantic surrounding them by a fringing coral reef. Grand Turk and its sister island Salt Cay have good beaches and interesting remnants of the old salt industry. The diving throughout the islands is as good as any in the Caribbean, with comparatively unspoiled reefs and some interesting wrecks around Provo going back to the early days of European settlement in the New World. Grand

Turk has quite spectacular wall diving a couple of hundred yards offshore where the shallow sea bed plummets to a marine trench two thousand metres deep – to swim out with mask and snorkel over the drop-off almost brings on vertigo as the crystal clear water shades from turquoise to ultramarine to black in the space of a few yards.

As my office and most of Government was on Grand Turk but almost all the tourism activity was on Provo I made the journey between the islands at least once a week. Usually I stayed in the small room at the back of Ron Ohliger's Ocean Club but once I tried Club Med. I introduced myself to the manager and stayed a night there to see what it had to offer. The location was the classic tropical island dream, the accommodation no more than basic, unimaginative bedroom blocks scattered through the palms. The evening was as I had expected, a mediocre communal meal, slightly tacky entertainment and lots of cheap liquor. At breakfast the restaurant host sent each arriving guest to the next available seat, all the identical tables seating 12. Any request to choose a particular table or set of companions was politely turned down. In Club Med, in the nicest possible way the guests are told what to do; it is apparently OK to get obstreperously drunk in the evening but at other times you follow the rules. I, in my turn was directed to a table. I asked the other 11 guests if they knew what country they were in. None of them did although one of them guessed 'Turquoise Island'. They had come to visit Club Med, not Providenciales or the Turks and Caicos Islands.

There was little that could be done with the limited tourism infrastructure on Grand Turk. The only almost-modern hotel was the Kittina, there were the couple of small dive operators and that was it. There was considerable room for improvement in the general environment. First impressions were terrible: there was a major litter problem, the low scrubby bushes festooned with discarded blue plastic bags, empty bottles and cans were everywhere with uncared-for feral donkeys rooting among them. Periodically the school children went on organised clean-ups but what was needed was some adult application.

It happened that there was a batch of confiscated under-sized illegally-fished lobster tails, frozen but badly stored and in danger of going off. A suggestion from the fisheries department that they be fed to hospital patients was rejected for the obvious health risk. The environmental health officer, Max, asked to be allowed to give them to the prisoners, who fed off them royally for several weeks. As a result they would do anything Max asked them, so he decided to have a drive to tidy the Islands, and out came a smiling and well-fed group of prisoners who collected most of the litter. He was known to the other TCOs as Mad Max but I considered him one of the sanest, and certainly most imaginative, people on the island.

While we developed a strategy to take the tourism industry forward, there was a bit of sorting out of the existing infrastructure to be done. I went through the complaints file at the Tourist Office. The hotel most complained about was the Island Princess, built in the 1970s at minimum cost by Cal Piper, one of Provo's Americans pioneers, and one of the most common complaints was about its primitive electrical wiring. A number of tourists had received electric shocks when trying to plug in their appliances and the place was obviously unsafe. I discussed it with Max, we discussed it with Cal, he decided the cost of bringing it up to an acceptable level was more than the hotel was worth so he closed it and sold the site. It was to remain closed for a decade, gradually taken over by the scrubby beach-front vegetation; it is now the site of one of Grace Bay's many condominium developments The Veranda.

I found the arrogance of the Club Med management offensive and thought they needed to learn a little respect for both the environment and the government of the nation which hosted them. Ron Ohliger told me that when Club Med had put down moorings for their dive boats, rather than obstruct the view for their guests they put them directly opposite the Ocean Club's beautiful beach next door. He had complained but had no support from the government, the Chief Minister being uninterested in a spat between foreigners on far-away Provo, so I formally asked Club Med to lift the moorings and re-site them opposite their own beach. They told me dismissively that with each mooring weighing 7 tons that was not possible. I told them that as they had managed to put them down, they would now manage to get them up again. Reluctantly, they did. Our relationship after that was less than cordial but as they did not consider themselves part of the islands' business community that did not concern me. Some months later, after the government had changed and Michael Misick was the new Minister of Tourism, I suggested that he meet with the regional director of Club Med to try to get them to buy into the new government's development plans. I was in his office when he was trying to arrange this; the local representative told us in his patronising way that his boss was a very busy man, he had 7 villages to run. 'Yeah,' growled Mike, 'and I've got a country to run.' The meeting eventually went ahead but Club Med never changed their ways.

* * *

Most of the tourism infrastructure and most of the development potential was on Provo where of the total population roughly a third were belongers, a third white expatriates mainly from North America and the remainder black expatriates, mostly from Haiti a hundred miles or so to the south. The concept of 'belongership' is one I have only come across in the Caribbean. It is looser than citizenship: it means broadly what it says, someone who belongs in the islands. This is usually by descent and includes the substantial numbers of Turks Islanders whose parents had moved to the neighbouring Bahamas, but the status can also be granted by the local government to non-citizens who are deemed by have contributed sufficiently to island life. Such grants are a considerable honour, officially gazetted and generally reported in the press; they allow the recipients to work and establish businesses in the islands. The concept has no official recognition in British law, while citizenship of a British Overseas Territory was, at the time of my arrival not quite what it would seem; it carried no right of abode in the UK. The blue British passport carried by Turks Islanders at the time did not entitle them to enter the UK without a visa, perhaps not quite the wonderful symbol of British values which Brexit supporters so longed for.

I visited Provo at least once a week. On my first such trip I visited Pine Cay, the old-established private island development. Life is full of strange coincidences: I met one of the residents, a Mrs. Smith, a middle-aged American alcoholic who had lived there for many years. Over a very enjoyable lunch we got to talking about yachts and I mentioned falling in love with one, the beautiful wooden 1930s-built Ticonderoga, when she had sailed into Copenhagen harbour some 30 years earlier as part of the centenary celebrations of the Royal Copenhagen Yacht Club. 'That was my father-in-law's boat' she told me.

Another early visit was for a few one-to-one meetings with individuals involved in tourism, very much a quick and informal trip. It was a hot day, I was dressed only in shorts and short sleeved shirt and in one of my meetings I was told that the Chamber of Commerce was having its monthly lunch that day and invited to attend. I sneaked in at the back, a little late, but was spotted. The Chairman said 'I see we have with us the new Director of Tourism who will say a few words'. I made my reluctant way up to the top table, in my short denim shorts, everyone else in business clothes. A voice from the back called out 'Hey, nice legs!' I tried to maintain my dignity, muttered a few words of thanks and melted back into the crowd, determined to wear long trousers to work in future. I later got to know the owner of the voice, one of TCIs more eccentric expatriates, daughter of a wealthy Canadian, who runs one of the liquor importers.

* * *

My initial contract ran for three months till the middle of April, a few days after my upcoming 50th birthday, and by mid-March we had made real progress. The office was running efficiently, enquiries were being responded to enthusiastically, I had persuaded Mitch, the longest-established dive operator, to do occasional shifts answering, with his cheerful enthusiasm, the 0800 number and we had adverts running in the major US dive magazines. Through our London PR agents we had invited a party of journalists to visit for a familiarisation trip, travel writers from The Mail on Sunday, The Scotsman and The Daily Telegraph plus a couple of freelancers; I had spent five days taking them around the islands, including visits to Provo, Pine Cay, North Caicos and Salt Cay. Provo was home to a dolphin rehabilitation project sponsored largely by The Mail on Sunday and one of the high points, for me as well as the journalists, was hand-feeding Rocky, the first dolphin to be taken on. By the end of the trip my nerves were worn to a frazzle - I was not cut out to be a tour guide ('could we possibly hurry up just a little? The taxi/plane/boat has already been waiting half an hour') but the trip gave us excellent publicity, including two double page spreads on successive weeks in The Mail on Sunday. There was one other outcome, a photo which I had taken was printed in a national daily: one of the journalists was very impressed by the Governors official car, a white London taxi, and I persuaded his chauffeur to drive it onto the beach where I photographed the journalist lolling against it, with an atmospheric backdrop of casuarinas. I asked that, in the event that the picture was used anywhere I should be credited as the photographer – I am a keen photographer but have never had anything published. When the picture duly appeared I was not credited, but as the paper in which it filled a quarter page was The Daily Telegraph, the one 'quality' paper to which I will not give houseroom, I was not unduly upset.

I had the enthusiastic support of the Board, all of whom wanted me to extend my contract by another three months so we could recruit a permanent director of tourism. As a formality I asked the Chief Minister to confirm his acceptance in writing and got a letter back saying that much as he appreciated all that I had done he was totally opposed to any extension of my contract. Doug told me it was political, the governing party automatically opposed most things initiated by HMG, but I suspected the influence of Norma, Skip's mistress, played a major part.

On what was meant to be one of my last Saturdays I decided to take the afternoon off and relax. I took my mask and snorkel and drove to my favourite beach on the South East corner of Grand Turk in search of conch shells to take home. I swam round the colourful coral heads just offshore, the water a little choppy and visibility poor, spectral barracudas emerging from the murk, checking me out then gliding away. I went beachcombing, found a couple of good conch shells and lay down in the shade of a small stand of casuarina trees to read the book I had brought. There was a family fishing in the shallow water about a quarter of a mile away, otherwise the beautiful golden beach was quite empty. Dotted along the horizon were the smaller cays of the Turks group, with Salt Cay, the only other inhabited island, in the far distance. Otherwise nothing but sea, sand and sky. I thought 'what a perfect site for a small hotel' but a big part of me said 'Why spoil it?'

On April 4th, a week or so before I was due to leave, there was a general election. Under the electoral system 13 members were elected to the Legislative Council, one or two of the constituencies having multiple members. I had moved in to The Saltraker for my last few days and spent the evening with Richard Stoneman, drinking in various bars and listening to the results as they came in; by the time the antepenultimate result was announced at around 11.30 we were back in the bar of the Saltraker with Jenny, the manager. The opposition People's National Party, PNP, were leading 6-5, needing one more seat for a majority; Jenny decided to go to bed, leaving us the keys to the bar with instructions to lock up. We had a few more beers waiting for the next result, the constituency of North Caicos where Mike Misick was standing, on which not just the election but also our individual futures in the Islands depended. We knew that if the PNP, led by Mike's oldest brother Washington, came to power there would be a totally different and much more focussed political landscape. There were several recounts and when the final result was announced sometime around 2.00 a.m. Mike had won by a couple of votes (the turnout was around 800), victory for the opposition: We gave a cheer, Richard headed home and I locked up, staggered to my room and finally got some sleep.

I had got to know Washington while working on the Mokoro study. I found him thoughtful and intelligent, a man with a clear vision for the islands; we became friends. The morning after the election, fairly hung-over, I had breakfast with him, by then officially Chief Minister, and asked him if he would extend my contract by three months, which he did without hesitation. I flew back to London a couple of days later, only just getting there in time to celebrate my 50th birthday: the American Airlines flight from Miami to London was overbooked and they ignored my plea for any sort of 50th-birthday preference but I managed to re-route myself via New York and got back to my family with a day to spare.

* * *

I returned a week or so later to a changed environment, a new government with new attitudes. Washy asked me for recommendations on members of the Tourist Board; I recommended replacing the Chairman, Josephine, with her marked racial inferiority complex, and the vice chairman Norma. When the decision was taken both ladies were in Miami, doing their shopping at the board's expense; by the time they came back Washy had gone off to Mexico for a conference. Small communities love gossip and scandal and Grand Turk was no exception. Word spread throughout the island that this new Englishman was shaking things up and trying to have two Turks Islanders removed from the Tourist Board. Before they had been officially notified Josephine and Norma heard of their removal on the grapevine, assumed I was the cause and refused to accept it. There were lost tempers, including mine, doors and telephones slammed and Bill vs.

Norma became the talk of the town. Norma was generally unpopular because of the terrible reputation of the old Tourism Office, not entirely her fault but everyone saw her disappearing off on overseas trips every few weeks and there was widespread jealousy. It had its comic elements: the cashier in the small supermarket whispering 'I'm with you, man' as she gave me my change, a stranger coming up to me in the streets to tell me she was praying for me. Finally the acting Chief Minister ordered Norma to take a couple of days compulsory leave, and I went off round the islands for some peace and quiet. Eventually things simmered down but from then on Norma would not talk to me. Fortunately I got on fine with the other four staff members and the office functioned better than it ever had.

On my return to the island I moved into a small pre-fabricated cedar-built A-frame house at Palm Grove, 10 minutes' walk from the middle of town. It was part of a development universally known as The Brown Houses, one of a dozen or so circled round a small swimming pool 50 yards back from the beach. It was light and airy, a double-height living room cooled by fans and two mezzanine bedrooms above the kitchen and bathroom and it became my home for the next three months.

Shortly after I returned my wife Bente came out to join me for three weeks, Emma being in boarding school. The morning she was due to arrive I had breakfast with Washington at The Saltraker. I was keen to make a good impression on the new Chief Minister to secure his support for what I and the Tourist Board wanted to get done. During the preceding months I had got to know all the Saltraker staff well; along with many of the expats both short and long term I was there a couple of times a week or more. Elaine, with her earthy sense of humour, was serving us and overheard me mention to Washington that my wife was arriving that day. She stepped back, feet apart, fists on hips, the very picture of a woman wronged: 'Yo' wife? Yo' wife? You didn't tell me you had no wife?!!' So much for good impressions. Satisfied with the look of shock on Washington's face she sashayed off with a broad grin. If nothing else it told Washy that I was becoming accepted in the community.

As Chief Minister Washington, with his background on Provo, had a vision for the islands and unlike his predecessor Skip he had the ability to deliver it. Richard, with some input from me, drew up a plan for a massive (by earlier standards) aid programme aimed at making the islands financially independent within five years based on the simple idea of government, including HMG, working together with the private sector – the norm in the past had been more confrontation than co-operation. The plan was called, appropriately, Progress through Partnership.

The islands had never been self-sufficient and the British Government representatives from Barbados, augmented by a Deputy Secretary from London, came to discuss this with a general attitude of scepticism. Washington and Richard made an impressive presentation. At some point the HMG team, who would have to sell the proposal to Whitehall, said that before they would agree they needed to see detailed five-year projections for the economy. 'No problem', said Washy. 'And Who's going to prepare them?' they asked patronisingly. 'Bill is' said Washy, to my considerable surprise. In all I had done in my varied working life up till then I had not ventured far from my accountancy roots with any degree of success. It is commonly thought that accountancy and economics are closely related. They are not, they require very different mind sets.

Partially as a result of those talks I was asked to extend my contract by another few weeks to help Washy set up his new ministry specifically to co-ordinate the development of the islands and before doing so I made a brief visit home. Driving my middle daughter back to university I told her that I had been asked to prepare detailed economic projections for a small island nation, a task for which I was completely unqualified. She, who throughout her life has treated challenges as opportunities, said 'Don't be silly, Dad, of course you can do it' so I returned to the islands to take up the unexpected challenge in a positive frame of mind: if my daughter Margaret thinks I can do it, I can do it. I set about preparing figures which would have to stand up to scrutiny in both Bridgetown and Whitehall. Not being a trained economist I resorted to common sense. I had got to know most of the influential private sector business people through the Mokoro study and my time at the Tourist Board and I interviewed many of them to get a feel for their own business plans. I knew which were pessimists and which were bullshitters: I upgraded the estimates of the former, downgraded those of the latter, and projected the composite picture onto the economy generally; perhaps not the conventional approach to economic forecasting but the resulting picture felt right.

As an aside, my projections and Richard's strategy proved to be spot on, and for some years after I set up the Tourist Board and helped shape the future path for tourism TCI consistently achieved the highest economic growth rates, not just in the Caribbean but in the whole of the Western hemisphere.

* * *

I had grown to love the islands. On my way back from a visit to Provo I stopped on South Caicos for their annual regatta. It was, of course, a warm sunny day. The centre of town, usually deserted, was alive with a thousand visitors who had walked there, sailed there or, like me flown in from other islands and on the quayside there were market stalls thatched with palm fonds selling food and drink and handicrafts. I knew many of those who were there and as Director of Tourism and one of the few expats who socialised fairly indiscriminately, was known to many more. I spent the day hanging out on the waterfront, drinking cold beer in the hot sun, grazing on the offerings of food, chatting with friends visiting from Provo, getting to know others, cheering on the participants in the casual boat races (everything on South Caicos is casual) and generally socialising across the spectrum. In the evening I was asked to be one of the judges in the 'Little Miss Regatta' contest for girls under ten, the five entrants all totally captivating little ladies with amazing poise and personality, and as I chatted with the two other judges I realised that I felt more at ease in this tiny and isolated community than I did back home in the outer suburbs of Surrey. As the only hotel was full I slept the night in the old District Commissioner's house, under renovation, the only furniture a bare bed and a couple of decrepit arm chairs. It stood on a low hill overlooking the town, with a 360 degree view of the sea, the surf of the Atlantic on one side, the calm of the Caicos Banks on the other; the house creaked like all old timber houses creak and was spooky with echoes from earlier centuries. I was well-fortified with the rum and beer I had enjoyed with new and old friends and slept the sleep of utter contentment. I woke late, less hungover than I deserved, wandered down the hill for breakfast in the hotel by the waterside then walked the quarter of a mile to the airstrip for my short flight back to Grand Turk to spend my last few days wrapping things up.

    I had completed my work at the Tourist Board by identifying and recruiting a full-time Director of Tourism, Clifford, a Bahamian of Turks Island extraction with extensive experience of hotel management and general tourism. Of course I felt a sense of loss, someone had taken 'my' Board away from me, but also a sense of satisfaction of having done the job to the best of my abilities. On my last Friday I was sitting at my laptop in my office just after midday when Pauline, Hyacinth, Sita and Talmadge came in with fried chicken, beer, a cake that Pauline had baked and a few other goodies and told me that I was lunching in! They had bought the chicken from The Poop Deck restaurant because I had told them weeks before that I liked it and Corona beer because they knew it was my favourite. I invited Norma to join us for lunch. Not surprisingly she refused but she made her presence felt by marching up and down the corridor outside my office, singing hymns very loudly, hymns which told her 'Jesus is the answer'! I am not sure what the question might have been.

I had had some tributes for the job I'd done but that lunch was the most touching. When I first arrived six months earlier the ladies were so shy they couldn't speak to me, they were completely unmotivated and hopelessly inefficient. By the time I left the office was alive, clean and tidy, all the equipment in full working order, the staff chirpy and friendly when visiting tourists dropped in and they had obvious pride in what they were doing. Pauline, large, shy Pauline, said 'We was plannin' to leave before you got here'. The fact that I got them a substantial pay rise helped but several people told me that it was because I made the staff feel important and given them some pride in their work. Certainly they were sufficiently confident to tease me at times: the day my wife, who I hadn't seen for weeks, was due to arrive I left early and as I had a breakfast meeting the next day I started to tell them that I would be late in. Pauline looked at me and said 'You plannin' to sleep-in late?' and dissolved into giggles!

On one of my last days as Director of Tourism I went for my early swim just after sunrise. There was a scrubby bank between the compound and the beach and as I climbed it I looked up and saw three wild horses standing under a casuarina tree. They heard me and turned their heads in unison. The wind lifted their manes and their tails and their silhouettes against the early morning sky with the sea as a backdrop is a picture that will always remain with me and that somehow captured Grand Turk as I wanted to remember it: not the scrubby, litter-strewn arid little island which it was but, to use the slogan coined by Clifford when he took over from me at the Tourist Board, Beautiful by Nature.

After I left the tourist board in Clifford's capable hands I was asked to come back for a few weeks to prepare a feasibility study for a small luxury hotel at Governor's Beach on Grand Turk. An architect, Guy Lovelace, the developer of the beautiful Windmills hotel on Salt Cay and designer of a number of other up-market hotels in the Caribbean, had done some sketches and I was tasked with getting it into a form to present to potential investors. I had visited Guy at Windmills a few weeks before. There were only a dozen rooms, each one very individual, with wooden furniture hand-made in Haiti, renting even then at $1000 per night. It sat at the top of as fine a beach as I've seen, with no other building within half a mile and was the perfect secluded hideaway – the visitors' book had many well-known names in it. It was built by hand using local labour employed and supervised by Guy. Concrete was mixed in a small mixer and delivered to where it was needed in buckets. During the construction Guy took his foreman, who had never before left the islands, to Miami to buy materials. On driving away from the airport the foreman looked at the interwoven concrete flyovers and said 'man, that's a lot of buckets'.

Sadly, although the proposal for the Grand Turk hotel had merit and looked to be financially viable those charged with marketing it were unable to interest potential investors and the lovely Governor's Beach remains even today without a hotel. Windmills was destroyed by a devastating hurricane in 2008: what had been lovingly built, bucket by bucket, is now an abandoned ruin being slowly reclaimed by nature.

* * *

The only major tourism development on Grand Turk since I left has been the building of a cruise ship facility, a jetty where passengers can be landed while ships are anchored offshore, fortunately in an area where there is no living coral, with a 'tropical paradise' pool and restaurant area onshore. I visited a few years ago and watched for a while as a couple of thousand people, mainly North Americans, bought hamburgers and fancy cocktails and enjoyed the Caribbean life of their dreams, which of course had nothing to do with the reality of Grand Turk. Outside the security fence, built more to keep the tourists in than the residents out, the few taxis on the island queued for the tiny number of visitors brave enough to take the two-mile drive to the town centre.

It was fascinating watching those who did. I was in the post office one day chatting to the ladies behind the counter when a small group of cruise-ship visitors came in. The conversation went something like this:

Dominant Female Tourist: 'I wanna stamp!' said with that inexplicable aggressiveness I've occasionally noticed in American tourists when out of their comfort zone.

Post Office Lady: 'Of course, madam. How much for?'
DFT, with exasperated expression: 'I wanna stamp for my passport!'

POL: 'You'll need to go to the immigration department for that. It's only a couple of hundred yards away.'

DFT: 'How can I find it?'

At this point I stepped in. 'I'm going that way myself, I can show you.' And then the weirdest thing: she looked right through me as if I wasn't there and the group left without in any way acknowledging my presence. I can only think that, as they had initially seen me talking informally to the staff they assumed I must be a local and therefore a simpleton not worth spending time or effort on.

A Turks Island friend of mine told of one tourist who did try to engage him in conversation: his opener was 'Tell me, is this island, like, completely surrounded by water?'

* * *

My time with the tourist board was a period of achievement, frustration and satisfaction during which I cemented my relationship with the islands. During my stay one of my sisters needed to contact me, on a Saturday afternoon, to give me the sad news that our brother-in-law had died of pancreatic cancer, tragically young and at the height of his professional career; all she knew was that I was in the Turks and Caicos Islands. She managed to reach the Cable and Wireless operator: 'I'm trying to contact my brother, Bill Samuel. Do you have a number listed under that name?' To which the operator replied 'I think I saw him going to his office a while back – I'll try there.' Only on a small island. Just before I finally left I called Cable & Wireless to arrange for my phone to be disconnected. The operator asked who was speaking. I said 'Bill Samuel' to which she immediately replied 'From the Turks & Caicos Tourist Board, how could I forget.' I had made my modest mark on the islands.

6. THE OFFSHORE FINANCE CENTRE

SOMETIME AFTER LEAVING THE TOURIST Board I was once more approached by the TCI government. I had, in the Mokoro Report, made the point that if the developing financial services industry was ever to rival that of the Cayman Islands it was essential for it to be both well-regulated and seen to be well-regulated. The long-serving Superintendent of Offshore Finance who had overall responsibility for banking, insurance, the company registry and related matters, had given notice that he planned to return to his native Zimbabwe and his chosen replacement would not be ready to take up the position for six months. Credibility would be lost if there were to be no one in-post so I was invited back to be interim Superintendent of Banking and Offshore Finance until the permanent appointee arrived; after an absence of a year I returned to the islands.

I recognised Turks Islanders as soon as I checked in for the flight at Miami airport. I received some warm greetings, in the departure lounge and on arrival, ranging from 'Welcome back! great to see you again!' from a government minister to 'haven't you been away somewhere?' from the myopic Peanuts with her cold box of drinks outside the ramshackle Grand Turk Airport building. My old house in Palm Grove had been standing empty since I left so I was able to move straight back in, greeted warmly, and hungrily, by the stray cats I used to feed. I called Cable & Wireless to have the phone reconnected, gave my name and the operator responded with 'Tourist Board, right?' It was good to be back.

The offices of the Offshore Finance Centre were above the Post Office on the first floor of a large white-washed stone-built 19th century building on the seafront. My office was a spacious, airy and cool room spanning the front of the building, with an uneven floor sloping towards the window, in which was mounted a noisy air-conditioning unit, used only during the hot months of June, July and August when the creaking ceiling fan couldn't cope with the humidity. It looked out west towards South Caicos, across the stretch of water shown on official maps as the Turks Island Passage. With accompanying PR this had recently been renamed by the TCI Government as the Columbus Passage in an attempt to boost Grand Turk's claim to be the first New World landfall of Christopher Columbus, the year being the five hundredth anniversary of his arrival. The sea was usually calm with little to be seen but one or two small traditional wooden sailing sloops with cargos of fresh fruit and vegetables from Haiti, clawing their way slowly up-wind in wide sweeping tracks between Grand Turk and South Caicos 20 miles away. A little later in the year there would be the occasional water-spout of the humpback whales returning from their summer feeding grounds off the coast of New England to mate and calve in the warm shallow waters of the Silver and Mouchoir Banks 50 miles to the south down towards Haiti.

On my first day I arrived at the office to find that my number two, the Deputy Superintendent and Registrar General, was also leaving. There were no plans to replace him so in addition to being Superintendent of Banking and having general oversight of the entire financial services industry I was also to be Registrar of births, deaths, marriages, patents, trade-marks and shipping - in a small nation one has to multitask. The newly recruited Superintendent of Insurance, who unlike me had specialist knowledge of his sector, was not due for a couple of weeks; until he arrived I would also be responsible for regulating the small offshore insurance industry of which I knew absolutely nothing. I had a secretary, Charlene, a delightful young Grand Turk lady whose father, a local lawyer who seemed to specialise in defending lost causes, I knew casually, there was a filing and accounts clerk and that was it. The company registry for which I also had responsibility was in a separate building close by.

As I was settling in on my first day, wondering where to start, Charlene knocked on my door, came in and said 'there's a lady outside wants you marry her'; I began to explain that I was already married then realised that, as Registrar General, I was also one of the official marriage officers and as such expected to perform marriage ceremonies. It gave me an idea of what to expect during the next few months.

At this point I started to write a layman's guide to the activities of international offshore finance centres, so-called tax havens, but it became boring and isn't particularly relevant to this memoir. I do however think it important to add a little perspective to the largely ill-informed media coverage generated by the publication of the Panama and Paradise Papers whose exotic names belie the dry legalese of their content.

Offshore finance centres come in for a great deal of criticism in our tabloid newspapers (mostly owned of course by rich men who treat the taxation regimes of the countries in which they reside with complete disdain and order their own affairs through the use of such centres). Much of this criticism is justified but some of it is uninformed and coloured by the picture conjured up by the name, small islands with white sandy beaches where shady characters can enjoy their ill-gotten wealth in tropical sunshine. The reality of course is different. Offshore finance centres exist primarily to allow international organisations to order their affairs unhampered by restrictions designed to regulate domestic activities.

The largest 'tax havens' include London, Hong Kong, Amsterdam, Luxemburg and Geneva, all of which help successful international businesses reduce their tax and regulatory burden on a far greater scale than any tropical island. London certainly launders more proceeds of crime than the Cayman Islands.

If TCI's offshore finance sector was to have any credibility it was important that the Superintendent, whose function was both to regulate and promote the industry, be respected by the professionals working within it and trusted by HMG. It was immediately apparent that my predecessor had been no different to many of the other TCOs, serving their time and drawing their tax-free overseas allowances while doing the minimum required to satisfy any of HMG's representatives from Barbados and Whitehall who occasionally dropped by. By the time I arrived he had already left, so without the benefit of any sort of handover it was up to me to try to find out how things worked or, in many cases, didn't.

I spent the first day meeting the handful of staff including those at the Company Registry and looking into the mass of paperwork generated by the various registries in those pre-computerisation days. My first explorations were not encouraging.

For most people in the government and the civil service the operations of the Offshore Finance Centre were a dark art only understood by those who had undergone complex initiation ceremonies; the two professionally qualified expatriates in charge had successfully kept at bay any outsiders who showed interest, projecting a façade of competence. Behind the façade was a mess almost as bad as that I had found at the Tourist Office: filing was months behind and two thirds of the 11,000 companies on the register were more than 8 months overdue in paying their annual fees with no system in place for chasing the delinquents. With an annual filing fee of $100 for each company there was well over half a million dollars overdue, a significant amount in terms of TCI's $35m annual budget. As I was to find out the lawyers and others who managed the companies on behalf of the beneficial owners were mostly very efficient: delaying paying over the annual charges in the knowledge that they wouldn't be chased for many months was a useful way of funding their cash flow – several of them had expensive small planes to maintain.

On the plus side I soon found out that by and large the staff, although overwhelmed by the volume of paperwork and demotivated by the lack of interest from my predecessor, were willing and competent, again echos of the Tourist Board.

Having responsibility for the banking sector of a British territory I had been told that my activities would be monitored by the Bank of England, whose agent in the Caribbean, Rodney, was notionally a consultant with what was then Coopers and Lybrand: international finance likes its cloak and dagger stuff every bit as much as the intelligence industry. I had had no training in banking or financial regulation and it should have been reassuring knowing that Rodney was available as there were times when I was decidedly out of my comfort zone. However I soon found out that he was almost impossible to find when I needed advice: I would telephonically scour the Caribbean for him without success and weeks later, unexpected and unannounced, he would breeze into my office, a tropical-suited financial Scarlet Pimpernel. This meant that for much of the times I had to make things up as I went along.

I settled into a comfortable routine, working long hours to bring the documentation up to date, flying over to Provo once a week to visit the professional community there and hosting monthly meetings of the Offshore Finance Committee, the members of which were drawn from the professional community. The contrast with tourism was great. Whereas the tourism industry is woven into the fabric of the islands, offshore finance sits outside everyday life. The lawyers and accountants making up the industry invariably dress as I used to when I had been a private sector professional, dark suits, formal shirts and always a tie (and yes, it was almost exclusively male). Having experienced the sophistication of financial services in London and Bahrain, even the Cayman Islands, there was, with a few outstanding exceptions, a slight air of children playing at being grown-ups. But that said they mostly appeared to make a comfortable living, with beach front or hill-top houses and of course their small planes. Some combined professional practice with real estate development; there were rumours, possibly spread by fans of John Grisham's excellent best seller 'The Firm' which had been published the previous year, that some occasionally used their planes for nefarious purposes but I never had hard evidence of that.

The weeks passed quickly, mostly routine but there were some memorable moments. Three characters straight out of a Damon Runyan short story, with garish sports jackets replacing black hats and white spats, visited my office to apply for a banking licence. I tried to let them know gently that the chances of it being granted were zero. To strengthen their case they argued that one of them already had a brokerage business and all client monies were kept with – they paused for dramatic effect - Paine Webber (at that time a leading investment bank) and 'they don't come much safer than that.' 'No', I replied, 'Paine Webber are probably as safe as Drexel Burnham used to be', Drexels being a top investment bank which had gone bankrupt the previous year, the largest victim of the collapse of the aptly named 'junk bond' market. Another pause while they searched their memories unsuccessfully for significant connections. 'Yeah, that's right' they muttered at last. That one I didn't need to run past Rodney: application rejected.

(As an aside my experience on the fringes of high finance have taught me that, for all the money they generate and pay themselves many of those involved are surprisingly gullible. They were surprised when financial instruments which the markets had christened 'junk bonds' turned out to be junk, just as, nearly 20 years later the sub-prime mortgages proved, in the financial meltdown of 2008, to be very much sub-prime. I have been fascinated by the centuries-long history of financial markets from the tulip mania and South Sea bubble of the 17th and 18th century right through to the present time and have a theory that the period between financial crises is approximately the time taken by the output of the top business schools to reach senior management positions.)

Another gentleman came to see me, introduced by the eccentric Tina from the Kittina Hotel. He was in his seventies, obviously down on his luck, and spent half an hour telling me of his recent business losses, expensive divorce and the bankruptcy of his business partner. When I suggested gently that he get to the point of the meeting, he said he wanted to apply for a bank licence. Again, application rejected.

Part way through my assignment one of the marriage officers visited my office with a gentleman who described himself as a widower, to whom we had issued a special marriage licence at a cost of $50. His wife, he had assured me, had died in Haiti but so far he had been unable to produce her death certificate. I suggested he go to Haiti to get a copy. He agreed, but then asked whether, in the event she wasn't dead, we could credit him the $50 until he could arrange a divorce. Marriage postponed.

During my time as Superintendent, in addition to births, deaths and marriages I registered a few dozen trade-marks for large multi-national companies, licenced a bank and struck off some companies which I suspected were engaging in nefarious activities in remote corners of the world; there was seldom a dull moment. I registered a couple of ships, one plying the seas of Indonesia, the other tramping round the Carribean; the TCI Register of shipping is considered to be British, lending a slightly misleading veneer of respectability, although I relied entirely on the British shipping registry in Cardiff for anything technical. Incidentally the trade mark and shipping registers were just that, large leather bound books showing the wear of many decades, with entries in ink. I also worked with the professional community and the attorney general to improve some of the legislation regulating the finance industry, important to its international credibility. I probably wore more different hats in the space of that six months than in the whole of the rest of my working life.

Midway through my assignment I had to return to London for the court case brought by my previous employer to retroactively change the terms of the agreement he had willingly signed after our discussions on my severance package; the effect would be to deprive me of my valuable and hard-earned stock options. It was in the Chancery division of the High Court and my lawyers, one of the leading City law firms, had assured me that my opponent's case was unwinnable; after nearly three years of very expensive litigation it was finally coming to court. It ran for three very stressful days, during which my opponent and ex-employer, an internationally respected banker who regularly attended the World Economic Forum in Davos, dismissed our signed agreement with 'but milord, I never read anything I sign.' The elderly judge who at times appeared to be sleeping and who clearly didn't understand much of the complexity of the financial world gave his judgement on the fourth day: to the surprise of both myself and my lawyers my opponent won. I found out later he had a reputation for siding with the establishment against the under-dog.

I've had a few unexpected and painful reversals as I've made my way through life and found that, no matter what, life will go on, this too shall pass. I returned home, my wife and I drank a couple of bottles of champagne which somehow seemed appropriate and a couple of days later I returned to Grand Turk, significantly poorer but with the weight of litigation finally lifted from my shoulders. There are far worse places in which to recover from a set-back.

After the ordeal of the High Court I was in serious need of some relaxation. It was October 1992 and the island was celebrating the quincentennial of the arrival of Christopher

Columbus in the New World. Several islands in the Bahamas claim to be his first landfall but the case for Grand Turk is sufficiently credible for it not to be dismissed. I unpacked, called in at my office to go through the mail then went down to town to join the Columbus celebrations. I stopped off at the Kittina and had a drink with Kit and Tina, unusually both there at the same time; While in the bar I got drawn into a political discussion with a couple of taxi drivers and an acquaintance from Provo who was visiting; after the be-wigged and hushed atmosphere of London's High Court it was good to be back in the real world.

I went on to the little square by the post office where there was an open air church service among the eighteenth century cannons, with perhaps a couple of thousand islanders including visitors from Provo and the Caicos islands, after which there was a fireworks display from a ship anchored just offshore. I had planned to enjoy the celebrations which followed but the very rapid transition from the pervasive damp of London's autumn to the heat of the Caribbean and from the daunting court hearing to this joyful celebration of such a pivotal event in history proved too much so, jetlagged and emotionally exhausted I went home to sleep.

The following day, the 14th of October, Columbus Day, had been declared a bank holiday, a day of celebration. The first official event was a slightly surreal recreation of Columbus's landing, on a beach which had been renamed Guanahani, the name given by Columbus to the island where he first encountered the Taino people. A group of visiting dignitaries from Cincinnati, apparently members of the Flat Earth Society and dressed up in period costume, landed from a yacht and stuck a flag in the sand, claiming the island for the King of Spain. Afterwards they wandered among us handing out beads, a few of which I was given by the lady Mayor of Cincinnati: she read out a proclamation declaring eternal friendship between the peoples of Cincinnati and Grand Turk. A bar had been set up at the top of the beach and I finished the day drinking Guinness with the Governor, each for our own reasons enjoying the opportunity to relax.

Eventually my permanent successor, a man with one of the most important requisites for the job, a great sense of humour, arrived. We had an enjoyable two week handover period during which I briefed him on both the wide-ranging responsibilities of his position and the quirks of the community in which he would exercise those responsibilities, happy to be leaving the job in better qualified hands than my own, sad to relinquish my office looking out over the blue Caribbean, with its slow parade of Haitian sloops bringing fresh fruit and vegetables and the occasional exuberant leap of a whale heading south to mate.

Having helped my replacement to settle in my final task was to carry out a short marketing study of the potential of TCI as a credible offshore finance centre, which I did under the auspices of one of the major London based consulting firms. Sadly their whole approach, typical of such companies, was how to leverage their first assignment in TCI into an ongoing stream of fee income. The resulting report, mainly written by the consultant from their staff with whom I had to work, who came to the assignment with little knowledge of offshore finance and left without significantly improving on that, is not something of which I am particularly proud so I will gloss over it. One memory however stands out: in the course of the study I had to visit Toronto to interview some members of the professional community, Canada for obscure reasons having strong links with TCI. My limited travelling wardrobe did not allow for this unplanned trip – it was late November, well below freezing in Toronto and I only had clothing for the tropics. I stopped off in Miami to buy a coat which would keep out the worst of Toronto's cold. Miami is not a centre of sartorial elegance, more influenced by its long-time resident Gianni Versace than Saville Row: all I could find was a full-length puffer jacket in a vibrant shade of purple. Wearing it I looked like a garish animated duvet but the professional community of Toronto was polite enough not to pass comment – perhaps I fitted their image of a representative of the Turks and Caicos Islands.

As the official banking regulator I thought I should have a formal sign-off at the end of my assignment: I tried unsuccessfully to contact Rodney, the unofficial but acknowledged Bank of England representative in the Caribbean. Throughout my time in the post I had had difficulty contacting him – this was before the age of mobile phones – and this attempt was no exception: I had to leave without completing this final formality. But true to his Scarlet Pimpernel persona he surprised me a few months later: I had moved on to my next assignment, a strategic review of the economy of Anguilla, and was relaxing in my hotel room after work when the phone rang: 'Bill, it's Rodney. I think you've been trying to find me'. 'Finally', I said, 'where are you?' 'I'm in the room next door!' So my final sign-off as Superintendent of Banking in the Turks and Caicos Islands took place over a couple of beers in a beach hotel on another small British Island also perched on the edge of the Atlantic but many hundreds of miles to the south.

During the two years since I had first set foot on Grand Turk I had invested much of myself in the islands, and the islands had given me much in return. I would have loved to stay on in some capacity, to continue to be involved, to see how they developed. The position of Chief Secretary, head of the civil service, was vacant so I applied, somewhat tongue in cheek, in the faint hope that the usefulness of my links throughout the community would be recognised and would outweigh my slightly subversive tendencies. Unsurprisingly my application was rejected, I was not to be the Robin Butler of the Turks and Caicos Islands, but my continuing connection with the islands came in the form of an offer from the private sector.

Through my work at the Offshore Finance Centre I had met Grethe Seim, the widow of a Norwegian shipowner Nils and owner of a small private bank. When Nils had retired they moved permanently from the bustle of Manhattan to the peace of Grand Turk. They had come across the island in the early 1970s and bought a house, standing high on the cliffs on the east side, looking out past Gibbs Cay to the endless expanse of the Atlantic. They had considerable wealth and initially banked with Barclays, the largest bank operating on Grand Turk, geared more to the day to day needs of the islanders than investment management for foreign millionaires. Eventually Nils became so frustrated with the poor service offered that he decided to set up his own bank, so in 1981 the Turks and Caicos Banking Company was born. He hired a young banker from Zurich to run it for him and promptly died, suddenly and unexpectedly, leaving Grethe as the sole owner of a small and efficiently-run bank catering to the needs of the wealthy.

She never remarried and was fiercely protective of her personal privacy, living alone in her beautiful cliff-top home, but she did involve herself in island affairs. She set up the Turks and Caicos Museum, initially on Grand Turk, later with an outpost on Providenciales, to showcase the many strands of TCI's mixed heritage, from the pre-Columbian Lucayan and Arawak settlements through to the present day. Its centrepiece is a collection of artifacts from the earliest European shipwreck found in the Western Hemisphere, on Molasses Reef a little south of the Caicos Islands. It is one of the best-curated small museums I have come across.

Every morning Grethe used to walk along the beach below her house where she collected things of interest, among them a surprising number of bottles containing messages, mostly arriving on the North Equatorial Current as it makes its leisurely way westwards across the Atlantic from the distant shores of Africa. Over the years she found and deciphered dozens of such messages, from the Canary Islands, Gibraltar, Lisbon and further: the longest journey was that of a bottle dropped over the side of a ship by an optimist travelling from Labrador to Greenland, which first floated east, then south down the coasts of Europe and Africa before turning west to wash up below Grethe's house 31 months later. Whenever possible she contacted the writers, a couple of whom visited from Europe. The collection is now housed in the Museum.

Grethe shared a love of golf with John Kelly, who became Governor in 1996, and together they designed a 9-hole course in the grounds of Waterloo, which was built for them by the prisoners who lovingly tended his rather arid gardens. It was undoubtedly one of the worst golf courses in the world, short, bumpy and stony but it offered Grethe the sort of challenge she enjoyed; it enabled her to indulge her hobby without having to visit the sink of iniquity which in her opinion was Providenciales, and allowed John to relax after work without resorting to the bottle, the curse of some of his predecessors.

While I was with the Tourist board I had met another Norwegian lady with a similar background to Grethe, who was developing a hotel on South Caicos. They were both very feisty Scandinavians with strong personalities. I once heard two Turks Islanders discussing them and the differences between them. One commented that in addition to sharing their nationality the two ladies had much in common. 'Yeah' said the other, 'but Grethe's got more Norwegiancy!' I knew exactly what he meant.

The Swiss gentleman running her bank, far from the social constraints of his native Zurich, was often to be found after work in the bars of the Turks Head or the Saltraker and Grethe, who had a strong puritan streak, did not have a good relationship with him. She was concerned for the confidentiality of the bank's affairs and after I left the OFC she approached me through her son and asked if I would join the board of the company as a non-executive director to generally keep an eye on the running of it. Of course I was delighted to accept, partly because with quarterly board meetings on Grand Turk I could continue to visit the island and partly because I had developed great respect for Grethe and enjoyed her company. Eventually my regular visits at the bank's expense led to the Turks and

Caicos government appointing me as their cost-free official representative in the UK.

* * *

I treasure the wide-ranging network of friends and acquaintances which life has given me and I enjoy connecting people who I think will get mutual benefit from knowing each other. Grethe's son Anders is a GP in Norway specialising in public health; he has inherited his parents' slightly unconventional approach to life as well as their philanthropic leanings. At the time he devoted a couple of days a week to his rural Norwegian medical practice and the rest of his time on a campaign to rid the world of guinea worm, then one of the scourges of tropical countries. The Guinea worm is a parasite, the larvae of which contaminate wells and streams and get into the bloodstream of those drinking from them. The worms eventually emerge from the host body through weak points on the skin, typically arm and leg joints, the effect of which is often quite crippling. Not being a killer it was not an infliction which attracted much funding, but neither would its eradication be hugely costly. All that was required was to instil in people the absolute necessity to boil or filter drinking water. Anders, single minded and determined, nagged the World Health Organisation in Geneva until they allocated him an office, arranged modest funding, I believe $20m, from the Jimmy Carter Foundation in the US and set up an educational programme which was hugely successful.

After some years the parasite had disappeared from most of the world's tropical countries, with its last major stronghold being in South Sudan where, torn as it was by a long-running civil war it was unsafe to send volunteers. Sometime in the mid-1990s a three month truce was declared to enable an attempt to negotiate peace and Anders immediately saw an opportunity. Because of my experience in East Africa he called me to see if I could help with logistics in Nairobi where he had decided to establish a temporary base. I phoned an old friend, Mansukh Shah, once a fellow member of Nairobi Round Table, an entrepreneur who owned a pharmacy and a factory making bandages. I hadn't spoken to Mansukh for 20 years but got an immediate 'Hey Bill-bhai, how's it going?' I put them in touch and got on with life.

Some months later Anders called me: 'Bill, Mansukh was fantastic. He immediately gave us an office, vehicles, a huge supply of gauze to filter water and all the logistical backup we needed.' Eventually the civil war resumed but sufficient inroads had been made to effectively complete the eradication. In 1986 there were 3.5m reported cases of guinea worm infection worldwide; by 2018 this was down to a mere 49 cases, spread across four countries. The Jimmy Carter Foundation takes credit for the eradication but it was brought about by the vision and determination of Dr. Anders Seim, a good man who continues to work on eradicable diseases in Africa through his Health and Development International Foundation. The following year Mansukh, another good and understated man, was murdered in his home by intruders.

* * *

There is much on the media about so-called tax havens and I realised how ill-informed our politicians are on the reality of offshore finance centres when I had a visit from a minister in the British government. He was taking a pre-retirement tour of the warmer British Overseas Territories at the taxpayers' expense, one of the expected perks of high office. He asked me how many companies were registered in TCI.

'Twelve to thirteen thousand' I told him.

'And how many of those are banks?'

'Eight'.

'Hm. I see. So there are eight thousand banks registered here'.

'No, there are eight banks registered here'.

This senior politician, at the time one of the richest men in parliament, was a member of a hugely wealthy family who are known to use offshore jurisdictions in their international financial arrangements. I doubt that he was any less informed on the matter than the average government minister, yet all of them still seem to think they are qualified to offer opinions on the unmitigated evils of the very complex activities of offshore financial centres.

7. DEVELOPMENT

20 YEARS BEFORE I FIRST came to TCI, living in post-independence Kenya I saw the benefits of an enabling government encouraging private sector development with minimal interference; there was a spirit of cooperation with individual ministers making themselves very accessible. The President, Jomo Kenyatta, stamped very firmly on any attempts at corruption (although sadly he exempted his venal wife Mama Ngina) and widespread corruption only came into Kenyan politics after his death; under his inspirational leadership the cooperation of ministers was driven by the wish for development rather than desire for personal gain.

During my time working with the Tourist Board and the Offshore Finance Centre the similarly supportive attitude of the TCI government elected not long after my arrival enabled me to play active roles in several significant developments.

Before the tourist industry could be developed to any significant extent it was necessary to address the two major impediments to development, the uncertainty of air access and the very limited infrastructure, particularly roads, on Provo.

When I arrived the only scheduled flights in and out

of the islands were operated by Pan Am, three a week to Provo and - at the insistence of the Chief Minister - two a week to Grand Turk, all from Miami. Pan Am had filed for bankruptcy early in January 1991 under chapter 11 which protected it from its creditors but allowed it to carry on flying, and Delta Airlines had begun negotiations to take over those parts of Pan Am's once huge network which were still operating. Flights continued to arrive while negotiations went on but Delta had indicated that our remote corner of the Caribbean region would not become part of its network. This was a potential disaster for the fragile tourism industry so Richard and I set out to identify and contact other carriers to try to persuade them to put on an alternative service. Marc Redt, the manager of the Ramada, a very experienced hotelier from the Cayman Islands, had contacts in both Cayman Airways and Continental and he, Richard and I flew to Miami to meet with them. Three of Continental's senior executives flew in from Houston and we met with them at the MIA hotel above the airport terminal. I took an immediate dislike to the man leading their team, who obviously had complete disdain for small Caribbean islands and I sensed that they were simply going through the motions, so when he asked me my background, rather than telling him I ran the Tourist Board I told him I was an accountant. 'A bean counter, huh?' he replied and ignored me for the remainder of the fairly brief and inconclusive meeting. I got modest pleasure a few months later when Continental also filed for bankruptcy – perhaps their own bean counters hadn't been up to scratch.

We went on to the Cayman Airways offices in downtown Miami where we were welcomed warmly but told that while they were interested in including TCI in their route network they doubted whether they could persuade their board unless the agreement included financial guarantees from the TCI government. Such guarantees would have to be backed by HMG as the Turks and Caicos Government's credit rating at the time wouldn't even have qualified it for a Visa card. There were other concerns, particularly around the very restrictive Bermuda II agreement governing air transport between the US and the UK which by a quirk of history extended to the British Overseas Territories. Fortunately we knew that a less-restrictive revision had already been drafted and was shortly to come into force so we persuaded them to ignore that. Richard, Marc, Lisa Agard and Hugh O'Niell, a Provo based lawyer, went to Grand Cayman to agree the details and returned with a deal subject to a guarantee which would kick in when any flight fell below the breakeven point of around 50% of capacity, subject to an overall limit of $500,000.

TCIG, whose liabilities are effectively underwritten by the British Treasury, could only agree if they had the blessing of the ODA representatives in Bridgetown. This they would only give if we could not only get commitments from the private sector to share the risk and meet half of any calls made but also provide proof that $250k had been deposited in a local bank. From their usual patronising manner they seemed confident that this was an impossibility.

A workable structure was devised, acceptable to the relevant government departments, parcelling up the guarantee into 50 units of a $5000 each. Together with Lisa whose pro-active approach to overcoming unnecessary restrictions had endeared her to the private sector, Richard and I set up a meeting of the Providenciales Chamber of Commerce to try to sell them the idea and get as many commitments as we could. We didn't hold out any great hope but when we arrived at 9 o'clock the room was already full, a hundred or more people crowded into the limited conference facilities of the Ramada.

Most of those present recognised it as a potential turning point in the development of the islands, the first major collaboration between Government and the private sector; it was a tacit recognition by the usually disdainful government on Grand Turk, of which all three of us were representatives, of the importance of Provo to the nation's overall development. Richard and I made the pitch, Lisa's presence as Attorney General adding a layer of comfort, and we invited questions. There was of course much debate on the actual level of risk, the security offered by the proposed structure which was to be administered by Hugh, a charming but slightly free-wheeling Irish lawyer, and the likelihood of the guarantees being called. Our hopes rose and fell during the long morning; we desperately needed the first person to commit and finally, after a couple of hours Sandy, the local head of Barclays Bank, agreed to take 5 units, a commitment of $25,000. His offer was quickly matched by Scotia Bank, Barclay's main rivals in the islands determined not to be outdone, and with suitable encouragement others began to commit. Ron with his Ocean Club up and running and his visitors depending on reliable air access committed early, as did Klaus who was about to break ground on the building of Grace Bay Club. Club Med of course didn't bother to attend, relying as they did on charter flights and considering themselves to be insulated from the problems faced by the industry. Most of the established tourism-reliant businesses took at least one unit, Chloe, Casablanca-born French travel agent and one of the pioneers on Provo, shared a unit with her mother, but by the time the meeting broke up we were still short by some $30,000. We collared the banks, the head of the Provo Power Company and Marc from the Ramada and they agreed jointly to make up the shortfall. It had been as long a five hours as I could remember.

While Hugh and Lisa completed the legal formalities I spent a couple of days at the Miami offices of Cayman Airways selling the attractions of TCI to their marketing staff and eventually, a few weeks before Pan Am/Delta withdrew their service, the first Cayman Airways 727 landed on Grand Turk. One hurdle cleared. When Pan Am finally stopped flying their well-remunerated agent on Grand Turk blamed me personally for the collapse of the long-established airline which had started life flying mail between Key West and Havana and risen to become one of the world's largest airlines; she never spoke to me again.

Lisa, a delightful lady of Trinidadian origins who had brought some creativity and imagination to the position of Attorney General usually held by time-serving lawyers, had a very relaxed approach to life which was brought home to me when we found ourselves once on the same flight from Provo to Miami. The flight was in the early afternoon and the unhurried check-in facilities at the mildly chaotic airport always opened early so that all the passengers would be processed in time. We followed the usual routine, flew over from Grand Turk in the morning, checked in then headed off for a very enjoyable and leisurely lunch. As departure time approached she picked up on the slight nervousness I always show when flight time is tight. 'Don't be silly', said Lisa in the beautiful sing-song lilt of her native island, 'they're not going to take off without the Attorney General and Director of Tourism' and of course she was right; we cut it fine and were the last ones to board but we made it. We'd had a few beers with our lunch and somehow it felt deliciously naughty.

The Cayman Airways service was not without its teething problems. When the ageing Boeing 727 which with its integral rear steps was specially designed for small airports with restricted facilities, landed for the first time at the ill-equipped but impressively named Grand Turk International Airport those rear steps refused to function. The only available set of steps was wheeled out but its platform was four feet short of the aircraft door; an enterprising member of the airport staff found a workaround. The tourists, mostly American, emerged from the plane to find they had to negotiate a small ladder before they reached the actual stairs. I suspect some of them were having doubts about their choice of holiday destination.

* * *

At that time the only tarmac road on Provo ran northeast from the airport along the spine of the island towards the small marina at Leeward, degenerating halfway into a rough unmade track. There were several major developments planned for Grace Bay on the north coast including a golf course with accompanying residential accommodation and several very upmarket resorts; these were exactly the kind of developments needed to attract those individual tourists whose visits bring most benefit to the wider community. The developers were all reluctant to go ahead if their only access was a dry and rutted track so Richard proposed making the very considerable investment in tarmacking several miles along Grace Bay. Historically roads had always been funded by the British and the local government's budget wouldn't stretch that far so the application went to ODA in Bridgetown. With the bureaucratic mind-set which had stultified so much development in Britain's overseas territories for so long, they asked Richard to justify the cost with a traffic count. He explained that as it was not a proper road there was hardly any traffic: they replied that as there was so little traffic a tarmac road was obviously not needed. Catch 22 at its best, typical of the pedestrian and at times obstructive mindset of the colonial administration. To break the logjam he proposed seeking private sector finance, if ODA would match it. They agreed, probably confident that such investment would not be forthcoming from the private sector, the operation of which they plainly didn't understand. Unknown to the ODA Richard had already discussed the idea with the seven major potential investors who had expressed their support; this was quickly converted into formal commitments for $350,000, ODA reluctantly matched that, the fine new road was built, another hurdle overcome, a very significant tipping point in the development of Provo's tourism industry.

* * *

The development of the proposed Sheraton hotel on a prime 42 acre site on Grace Bay was mired in the complexities of its ownership. The project had been set up in the late 1980s as a tax shelter investment for a group of 50 Canadian dentists, with a performance bond issued by Zurich Insurance guaranteeing completion. Funds had run out when the building was only half complete, Zurich were refusing to pay on the guarantee and the company with its large group of poorly represented shareholders didn't have the capacity to fight them. No other developer was prepared to take it on until the financial complexities were sorted out so it remained, a gradually decaying eyesore on one of the most beautiful beaches in the Caribbean.

I had by then moved on from the Tourist Board to the Offshore Finance Centre. As there is considerable synergy between an upmarket tourism industry and offshore financial services I continued to take a great interest in the direction tourism was taking; although at times in my life I had made a good living in financial services I find people far more interesting than money and tourism is all about people. Fortunately at the OFC I was responsible for all insurance regulation, my workload by then wasn't too stressful and I had official stationery with an impressive government crest on the letterhead so I decided to take Zurich on. I wrote to them formally, suggesting that defaulting on the performance bond would severely damage their reputation, not just in TCI but internationally and to my pleasant surprise they capitulated comparatively easily, met their obligations, the dentists sold the development on and a couple of years later the new owners did a deal with Butch Stewart, the Jamaican founder of the Sandals resort chain. It became the first of his new Beaches child-friendly all-inclusive resorts. What had been an eyesore is now a beautiful development and an important part of Provo's tourism industry.

* * *

While all this was going on a number of entrepreneurial Turks Islanders were seizing the opportunities which presented themselves. Until tourism started to happen most families in the Caicos islands made a subsistence living from fishing or farming, little changed since their ancestors escaped slavery a couple of centuries earlier. Now their children had other opportunities open to them. I came to know many who have enjoyed considerable success; within a single generation Turks Islanders achieved, largely by their own efforts, a transition which had taken most families in the UK a century or more. A nation which HMG had despaired of, led by the private sector which many in government failed to understand, had raised itself from nineteenth century subsistence to late twentieth century affluence.

The opportunities were also open to those who

migrated from neighbouring islands. One of the key figures in the development of the island's aviation came as a young man from Haiti, the poorest nation in the Caribbean, learnt to fly and built up a large and successful business including an airline offering scheduled services throughout the region and an airport facility serving the executive jet market. As I write the current Governor has just appointed him to the National Assembly. It is said that success breeds success: the successes of the early pioneers on Provo led to a spiral of development which benefitted the entire nation, a fact even recognized, if grudgingly, on Grand Turk.

When I first arrived in the islands the view of HMG appeared to be that TCI would remain financially dependent on the UK indefinitely, that the local government was most interested in looking after its small power base of Grand Turk and the chances of any significant change were small. The British Development Division in Barbados, ever nervous of ambitious politicians, seemed to be more interested in blocking development than promoting it and to take the view that, despite Washington Misick's enthusiastic vision nothing would change. A few determined people proved HMG wrong. By identifying, addressing and unlocking the major constraints, a virtuous circle of growth was established. The nation was motoring and there were enough people with a stake in it to make sure development continued. For the following decade TCI saw one of the highest levels of growth in the world, matching those of China, and GDP per capita in real terms is now more than three times what it was in 1990.

8. MORNING COMMUTE

IN THE TROPICS DAWN COMES quickly, with none of the long, slow build-up of northern climes. The day arrives, more or less fully formed, at around 6.30 with little year-round variation.
I get up with the sun, put on swimmers, sandals and a tee shirt and feed Big Tom before heading for the beach some 50 yards away. When I moved into the house all the stray cats in the area came calling; being on my own and occasionally lonely I was a soft touch and fed them all but one day Big Tom, a large furry black feline thug, arrived and muscled his way to the bowl from which several of them were already feeding. When they had all backed off he disappeared briefly, returning with his scrawny little lady friend and kept the others at bay while she ate her fill. He then ate and escorted her into the house, leaving the scraps for the others. She lay down to sleep and he curled himself protectively around her. I had got myself a couple of cats, company for Richard's dog Tashy who I had inherited from Richard when he finally left the island.

The path to the beach runs over the low bank beside Sandy Lightbourne's house, currently rented to Rita from the Department of Sport and Culture. Sandy, originally from South Caicos, was the manager of Barclays Bank when I first arrived but is now living on Provo where he runs Lord Ashcroft's Belize

Bank. On the beach I chat briefly with Rita, out for her usual early morning walk, before donning my swimming goggles and heading out towards the reef some 200 yards offshore. Guiding me out is a tiny pilot fish, swimming a few inches in front of my nose and I wonder, as I do every day, if it is always the same one. Occasionally I pause, with my face below the surface, and scan for barracudas, not from fear but because I love their sleek form and their curiosity. Ian Fleming gave barracudas a bad name but in 35 years of scuba diving I never met anyone who has known anyone who has been attacked by one.

A few years later on one of my visits back to Provo I saw Rita at the airport talking to mutual friends and went over to say hello. As I approached she looked blank, then recognition dawned: 'Hey man! I didn't recognise you with your clothes on!' Years later we marched together in the opening ceremony of the Commonwealth Games in Manchester. We remain in contact: she was recently awarded the OBE for services to sport in TCI.

I return to the house for a light breakfast then set out on the 10 minute walk to my office. I leave the compound by the path next to Phil Johnson's large house; Phil is the entrepreneur who built the dozen A-frame houses using prefabricated kits which he imported from his native Canada some years before. I pick up the dusty road and head north towards town. On my right is a small salina, fringed with a few straggly reeds and grasses, home to various wading birds and visited by an occasional pelican or flamingo. On my left is the little block of 'town houses' built by Reg Bodanya, senior partner in the TCI branch of a smallish UK accounting firm, with funds reputed to have been 'borrowed' from the company's clients' account. Reg later had the distinction of being the subject of a TV documentary in the UK; the last I heard of him he was serving time in prison in California for mail fraud.

Further on I pass David Bagley's house, with his motor cycle and sidecar combination parked just inside the low wall of whitewashed coral blocks. David is the much-loved

GP, performing semi-miracles with very limited facilities, the nearest properly equipped hospital being some 600 miles away in Miami. I last saw him and his wife Sue when I bumped into them unexpectedly, years later, at a reception at the Governor's house on the small mid-Atlantic island of St. Helena. The revolving population of skilled expatriates working in the British Overseas Territories move comfortably between very different small islands. Grand Turk is very much a 'tropical island', St. Helena, closer to the equator, is not; no palm trees or white beaches, only misty mountains and rugged moorland.

The bushes dotting the scrubby ground around the salina are festooned with blue plastic bags; it must be a while since the schoolchildren did one of their occasional clean-ups. I can't seem to get the message over, that Grand Turk will struggle to get any significant numbers of tourists while it presents as an uncared-for mess. Cliff Hamilton, who has succeeded me as Director of Tourism, is using the slogan 'Beautiful by Nature' to promote the Turks and Caicos Islands in the international tourism market; he could add 'but messed up by people'.

I meet a feral donkey coming towards me, one of the many which wander the island at will. They are descendants of those that arrived in the eighteenth century to work in the salt production industry, a significant part of the island's history. During the war production had continued but the export was constrained by the constant threat to shipping in the Atlantic. One of the elderly British expatriates with whom I have an occasional beer told me that he had originally been sent to the island to arrange the sale of the accumulated three-million-ton stockpile. He managed to sell it all to Japan in a deal which involved barter of some kind and from which Grand Turk saw little benefit. Most of the donkeys are unpleasant, bad-tempered and capable of giving a nasty bite, quite unlike the cute cuddly animals pictured in adverts for donkey-sanctuaries in Devon. I avoid them.

I continue on past the old Kittina where I know tall, skinny, unsmiling Ivy will be serving breakfast to the handful of guests, most of them visiting on government business. On my right is the original part of the hotel, lovingly built stone by stone by Kit Fennimore, a retired US army sergeant with a reputation for bare-knuckle fighting, and his wife Tina, daughter of a general in the army of the Dominican Republic. On the left is the new block which they built a few years ago with a loan arranged by HMG when modern accommodation was needed for the entourage of Princess Alexandra who visited in 1988. The income from the hotel funds Kit and Tina's comfortable life in Coral Gables on the southern edge of Miami where they now live and where I occasionally stay when passing through, Coral gables being the nicest part of Miami – there is little competition. So far they have made no attempt to service the loan.

Past the Kittina on the left, between the road and the sea, are a pair of houses occupied by elderly couples of Bermudan ancestry. Although there are now few class distinctions on the island the Bermudans, descended from people who arrived of their own free will, seem to consider themselves slightly better than the darker-skinned descendants of slaves.

The road now skirts the beach and on my left are all the clichés of a travel agent's brochure. The sand is golden, studded with coral outcrops; inshore the sea is turquoise freckled with sunlight, further out a rich deep navy blue. In the far distance a small sailing sloop laden with fruit from Haiti tacks its leisurely way in towards the town jetty. A few large casuarinas susurrate in the breeze, offering shade from the sun, now beginning to release its heat. On my right set back among the trees is the Saltraker, converted years ago by Doug and Angie from a large old nineteenth century house into a charming small hotel. In its secluded courtyard restaurant Elaine, large and extrovert, the polar opposite to Ivy, is in charge, serving a handful of tourists visiting for the diving. Next door Cecil is outside his dive shop readying the tanks for the morning trip out to the reef where a handful of lucky visitors will get to admire the beautiful soft corals of the Caribbean. A little further on, on a platform built up over the beach is the restaurant set up a couple of years ago by X's ex-wife and ex-mistress when they had tired of his moods and his drinking. X's own restaurant, with its red English telephone box outside is fifty yards or so inland facing the large salina. X may be moody but he is both a good chef and a talented artist, his antique-style maps of the islands gracing many a T-shirt bought by tourists. The food at both restaurants is excellent.

The road, which has now become Front Street, narrows into a little lane, with the old Turks Head Inn sitting in its large and shady garden on the right, the office of the Misick and Stanbrook law firm on the left, seaward, side. Ariel Misick is a brother of Washington and Mike, a delightful man with a formidable professional reputation; his partner Clive Stanbrook has a legal practice in Brussels. Almost next door is Grethe's Turks and Caicos Banking Company where Anton will be digesting the latest financial data streaming in from the Bloomberg network to the bank's own satellite dish outside.

I continue down past the Cable and Wireless office with its far larger satellite dish and tall telecommunications tower whose metal latticework makes an ideal observation platform for the resident osprey. Barclays Bank is next door; I went in there the other day to be greeted warmly by the manager – I hadn't been in for a while. 'Hi Mr Samuel, how's things with you? What can we do for you today'. I told her I needed to transfer some money back to my bank in the UK. 'OK. We'll need photo ID for that'. Sometimes I wonder why common sense is so often subjugated to procedure.

Just past the bank, down below the sea wall, by now quite substantial and shoring up the road, is the small triangular beach where I used to swim before and after work when I was running the tourist board and staying in Doug and Angie's peaceful little guest flat. On my right is the lane that leads to their house. And finally I come to my office, on the first floor above the Post Office. It is an early nineteenth century building of hand-butchered coral blocks, whitewashed and bright in the morning sunlight. I climb the rickety wooden stairs clinging to the outside, into the small hallway then on through to my large, cool office which takes up the entire front of the building, its uneven floor of beautiful old planks darkened with age, sloping down towards the window. I turn on the fan which creaks into action, stirring the air which still carries the cool of the night. I scan the ocean for whales but there is only the single Haitian sloop which has made little progress since I first noticed it on my swim so I settle down to my interesting but undemanding work overseeing the small financial services industry of this almost unknown little nation on the edges of the Atlantic Ocean.

As commutes go that takes some beating.

A couple of years earlier my commute in Bahrain was also about 10 minutes, in an air-conditioned Volvo with Toni Childs at full volume. It was also beside the sea, but there were no low whitewashed buildings, only shiny modern high-rise, one of which housed the investment bank of which I was an executive director. I muse over the contrast: there I only had status because of my position, here I have become part of the fabric of this small Island community where everyone knows everyone else and there are few secrets. I much prefer here.

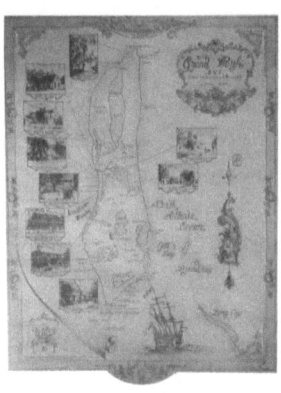

9. ISLAND LIFE

SMALL ISLAND COMMUNITIES ARE NOT dissimilar to isolated rural villages; everyone knows everyone else and most people are, in one way or another, related. If that island happens to be the capital island of a nation state still effectively dependant on its old colonial ruler there is an added layer of society which lives its life largely outside that of the general population: this is the expatriate administration sent by the ruler, which acts as much to protect the reputation of the ruler as in the interests of the local community.

A short term visitor living and working on such an island has two choices: to stay in the expatriate bubble, mixing socially only with others on short-term assignments and having minimal personal interaction with the local community, or to become part of the chaotic mind map that is small-island living, finding connections, seeing them double back on themselves, enjoying and using the frequent overlaps between work and private life. As someone who enjoys social interaction I chose the latter.

Although there are cars on the island most short journeys are on foot, which influences the character of the islanders: occupants of a car are largely isolated from those around them whereas pedestrians interact; with the love of gossip common in most closed communities people know more about everyone else's lives than they would in a more motorised society.

I discovered early on that the character of Turks Islanders is significantly influenced by the island in which they grew up. Salt Cay, with a population at the time of perhaps a couple of hundred, had in the 1970s and '80s only one school teacher but she did her best to ensure that her pupils left the small school with not only a broad education but with ambition and self-confidence; this showed in the success of many of its natives and the island, in itself a sleepy little backwater, punched well above its weight in the life of the nation. Grand Turk, as the seat of government and home of the civil service, pretty much guaranteed all its residents a job, leading to a slightly complacent attitude. Providenciales, set on its own trajectory far from governmental influence and the forces of law and order, had a frontier feel about it, attracting entrepreneurs and wheeler-dealers, both local and expatriate, who soon eclipsed the indigenous fishermen and irrevocably changed the nature of the island. South Caicos, still the centre of the fishing industry but heavily tainted by its involvement in the drug trade during the 1980s had a more lethargic if slightly piratical air. The people of North Caicos, which with its fertile soil and extensive underground freshwater lens was largely agricultural, had the respect which all farming communities have for their land: litter was far less in evidence than it was on the other main islands. Middle Caicos, although the largest inhabited island was a tiny village of a few dozen people, who had little contact with outsiders and all the shyness that brings. These are of course sweeping generalisations with many exceptions but it helped in my understanding of island life and the contributions of the different communities. On meeting someone new I would often open the conversation by asking what island they were from and what their family name was, which occasionally embarrassed anyone I was with but did not seem to give offence: most were proud of the heritage of their own particular island and the information gained helped build my composite picture of the community.

* * *

On Grand Turk the social life of the four thousand inhabitants was centred on the seven Christian churches – no other religions were represented. These covered the entire spectrum of Christianity from the very traditional Anglican and rather less traditional Roman Catholic to the evangelical, heavily influenced by the deep south of the United States. To improve my chances of being accepted by the local community I began to join in their Sunday worship and each week I would visit one or other of the churches for the regular service. I soon realised that just as life on a small island seems to exaggerate political views and divisions so it does with the characteristics of religion. The churches with British progenitors were all some way to the right of their parent. The Anglican had far more ritual, the Methodist felt more like conventional Anglican; in none was there the quiet contemplation found in British Methodist or Baptist churches and certainly nothing similar to the Quakers.

As a child I had been brought up in the Anglican tradition; I was confirmed while at school and accepted the 'truths' of the church as did most people from my middle-class background. Living in Kenya I had drifted away from religion and its rituals while retaining a belief in the spirituality of life: it is hard not to have a feeling of some divine purpose when standing on the top of Kilimanjaro watching the sun rise over Africa. By the time I arrived in TCI, with the strength of my marriage beginning to slip away I had turned back to the church for support, and while I no longer believed in Christianity I drew comfort from those who did.

The church I visited most often was the Bible Baptist, an offshoot of a church in the southern United States, housed in a large, barn-like structure in the middle of town. It was led by Pastor Fred Braithwaite, an ex-policeman originally from Barbados who had lived on Grand Turk for more than 25 years. In his own words he had been, in his youth, a real sinner but eventually saw the light and became a totally committed Christian, warm, charismatic and much loved by his small congregation. There were 40 or so worshippers each Sunday, many of them originally from other islands in the Caribbean who moved largely in their own supportive expatriate community - islanders around the world, including many in my home island of Great Britain, are not particularly welcoming to immigrants: Turks Islanders are no exception. There were always many children, the girls dressed in brilliant colours with their hair braided with beads, the boys in suits and ties, moving easily from one adult to another. The music was provided by Mrs Tatum, a light-skinned lady of Bermudan ancestry, handsome and matronly with thick pebble glasses and grey hair pulled back into a severe bun; she thumped away on the keyboard with a style that owed more to New Orleans than to any church I knew. She was sometimes joined by a young man on trumpet and another on guitar. The singing was full of joy, dominated by the women with the characteristic sharp timbre of the Caribbean and was led and controlled by Mrs. Tatum. When she paused for breath, we all paused for breath.

Early on I sat through a long and fiery sermon delivered by the leader of the parent church in South Carolina on one of his regular visits, officially to show support to this distant offspring but I suspect more to check that the strict Bible Baptist doctrine was being adhered to. His topic was the core belief of his church, that the King James bible was the only true word of God and all other versions were a corruption of the devil, where 'Satan slipped in a word here, a word there' till the true meaning was lost. I thought of my wife, brought up in the Lutheran traditions of Denmark where they never had a King James and so in the preacher's view were at the mercy of the devil. Religious dogma has many such illogicalities. (Years later I was reminded of this when a story, one hopes apocryphal, was circulating about President George W Bush: when asked why he spoke no foreign languages he supposedly replied 'if English was good enough for Jesus Christ it's good enough for me'.) But illogical as this belief was the community which embraced it was warm and welcoming to me even though as a white European I was an oddity. The faith of the congregation was very moving: I went one evening to a midweek prayer meeting in support of Joy, a young mother who was going to Nassau to be treated for cancer. We were no more than a dozen people and she stood in front of us, a single spotlight lifting her out of the semi-dark, tall, beautiful and slim as a reed. She sang to her lord, asking for his help, her voice hauntingly melodic and I was intensely moved. The tiny congregation offered their prayers, to no avail: she died in Nassau a few weeks later.

Although Pastor Braithwaite's church became my regular Sunday morning 'worship' I visited most of the others, from the formal and ritualistic Anglican to the very evangelical New Testament Church of God. Even by local standards the latter was fairly extreme. I described a service in my journal at the time:

'I'll set the scene: a small whitewashed building, windows open to the elements, fans creaking round in the ceiling; probably 120 people, mostly women, all in their Sunday best, brilliantly coloured dresses with lace and frills, elaborate hairdos or exotic hats; children walking round in dresses of velvet and sequins, their hair braided with beads and fluorescent ribbons. The music is a keyboard, two electric guitars, a set of drums and two people with cymbals; in addition several in the congregation have tambourines. The service is all singing, praising the Lord, hallelujahs, some communal bible reading and occasional speaking in tongues. The singing, powerful, beautiful and emotional, sent shivers down my spine and kept stopping me short with a lump in my throat. A few people sang solos which wouldn't have disgraced a concert hall. Lots of arm-waving, swaying and clapping of hands. Half-way through we all went round greeting each other - I started with the British handshake but soon found the bear-hug was the done thing. To my surprise I was not made to feel an outsider or an oddity, even though, apart from my friend Barry who goes regularly, I must have been one of the very few white people who have been to the church; I was welcomed as was any other visitor. The service lasted an hour and forty minutes, and I came away emotionally exhausted.'

One evening over a beer in the Turks Head I mentioned my rota of church visits to an Irish Catholic lawyer friend, he who had once dispensed justice from the back of a donkey and he said 'I bet you never visit my church.' He was right: I thought about this and realised how deeply rooted in me was my Anglican antipathy to Roman Catholicism and how unjustified prejudices can be instilled into children, never to be dislodged. I could accept and tolerate the absurdity of the core belief of the Bible Baptist Church but not the 1500-year-old traditions of Catholicism. His church was one of the least traditional, being housed in a flat above an office almost next door to the bar in which we were drinking.

In November 1992 I attended, in my official capacity as Superintendent of Offshore Finance, the Remembrance Day service on Grand Turk. The Anglican Church is a small stone-built 19th century building standing at the top of the beach looking out over the ocean. It had been freshly whitewashed for the occasion and most of the island dignitaries were there, the Governor being last to arrive in his official car, the white London taxi pretending to be a Rolls Royce. He was of course in full gold-braided dress uniform. The police band, smart in their peaked caps and white uniforms edged with red, marched the few hundred yards from their headquarters. After the service the congregation moved outside for the playing of the last post. It was extraordinarily moving, standing in the hot Caribbean sun on a small square of scrubby grass beside the ocean, far removed from the battlefields of Flanders. The national flag was at half-mast and the Governor, in his ostrich feather hat, read the very moving 'at the going down of the sun and in the morning we will remember them'. He doffed the plumes as the last post was played; the solo trumpeter, more used to the informality of jazz than the strict requirements of such a solemn occasion, struggled gamely with the unfamiliar music, getting most, but not all, of the notes right. The event hovered somewhere between Graeme Greene, Somerset Maugham and Tom Sharp and I was torn between tears and laughter, eventually giving in to both.

* * *

While I was working in the islands my then wife Bente, who had had some training in personal counselling, visited from time to time. When she first arrived on Grand Turk and began to get to know people she formed the opinion that with their long history of dependency the islanders had an identity problem and would benefit from some counselling. I had introduced her to Washington and she suggested to him that she start at the top, counselling the Government ministers. Washy, ever tactful, headed her off and said it would be more productive to start at the very bottom of society, in the prison; he introduced her to Pastor Braithwaite who also acted as prison chaplain. From then on, whenever she was on the island she spent much of her time in the prison, initially counselling the prisoners, later, at their own request, the prison officers. This is not the place for my opinions on the benefits of and sometimes harm done by the largely unregulated profession of counselling: her regular visits to the prison, getting to know the prisoners and letting them talk about themselves and their often troubled backgrounds undoubtedly changed the atmosphere within the prison very much for the better, as I was told much later by the UK-based inspector of prisons for the Caribbean. The prison was home to 50 or so offenders, including rapists, murderers and drug dealers; not once was she insulted, offended or made to feel unwelcome.

The prisoners had their own religious service every Friday officiated, if that is the right word for such unconventional worship, by Pastor Braithwaite and one week I decided to attend with my wife. It was very moving and slightly surreal. The old prison has since been replaced by a larger modern facility on the other side of the island but at that time it was right in the middle of town, housed in a small rectangular compound of perhaps a quarter of an acre between the sea and the salina, surrounded by high, whitewashed stone walls topped with barbed wire and broken glass. Entrance was through an imposing set of wooden doors some ten feet high with a huge Victorian cast-iron knocker, which looked for all the world like the entrance to the castle in the wonderful Mel Brook's film Young Frankenstein. Bente knocked; after a couple of minutes the door swung open, rusty hinges creaking, and we entered the sandy yard in which the prisoners were scattered, some playing dominoes or basketball, some reading, some just staring into space. In the centre was a covered area, a few posts supporting a roof of corrugated iron without walls, a pool table at one end and three short rows of benches at the other. Gradually Bente's 'clients' gravitated towards us, slightly nervous of me, and we started talking. They ranged from little old Hilton, in his sixties, a serial offender and perpetual victim of life who told me that Bente was like a mother to him, to Obed from North Caicos via the Bahamas, erudite, educated and an impressive and powerful personality. After a while Darren, a young white American preacher who was staying with the Braithwaites, arrived and we had our service. Only a dozen men, but they sang their hearts out, all the old hymns I had grown to love from my Ella Fitzgerald records, The Old Rugged Cross, Amazing Grace, Abide With Me and one that had become my new favourite, It Is Well With My Soul. The very simple beauty of it was intensely moving, a dozen newly-saved souls praising their Lord and a couple of dozen more hanging round in the yard not quite daring to participate, perhaps, having been brought up on the fire and brimstone of the Old Testament, sinners fearful of the judgement of God. I felt very privileged. One way or another, what I think of as my soul had taken a bit of a bruising among the glass and concrete towers of the Arabian Gulf: it was being healed in the strangest of ways among the whitewashed old stone buildings of the Caribbean.

A couple of weeks later we were driving home from lunch with friends one typically quiet Sunday afternoon, the road hot and dry and dusty, no other vehicles and no-one about until we rounded a corner and came across a line of prisoners ambling along the road escorted by a couple of prison warders known to Bente. 'Where are you taking them', she asked. The warders looked mildly surprised; 'It's Sunday, their day for the beach'! Since the treatment of prisoners was not particularly indulgent I can only assume that it was cheaper for them to perform their ablutions in the sea than for the government to build a decent shower block.

Eventually I got to know some of the prisoners quite well. Obed, who had been at the church service and was released shortly after, took to visiting us. He was a powerful man who had once represented the Bahamas in athletics, moody but intelligent and well-informed and he and I would discuss politics and play chess late into the evening, late on Grand Turk being 9 o'clock. We were fairly evenly matched and I enjoyed his company, eventually helping him set up a small business making concrete building blocks. He seemed a nice man but looks can be deceptive: he eventually re-offended, his crime both times being the violent rape of his teenaged step-daughter. Clyde was less complex, mild-mannered and a skilled mechanic. He wanted to put his time in prison to good use and I bought him by mail order a comprehensive toolkit which enabled him to set up a small business servicing the motorbikes and outboard engines owned by the prison officers. When he was eventually released he relocated the business to a proper workshop doing much the same thing on the outside. Many years later when I was visiting he introduced himself to me in the street – I no longer recognised him – and thanked me for helping to put his life back on track. Some you win, some you lose.

Shortly before we left the islands the prisoners put on a concert for us. We were formally invited, turned up at the allotted time, hammered on the big old doors and were escorted through to the corrugated-iron shelter where the church benches from my previous visit had been removed, replaced by just two chairs. We duly took our seats and the five-man band played for us. There was an oil drum, a tea chest and various kitchen and garden implements but not a single recognisable musical instrument yet the music they produced was thrilling – I've tried to find another word but that's the one which keeps presenting itself. I spoke to them afterwards and was told that music was one of the things which made their situation bearable and I could imagine that two hundred years earlier their ancestors, slaves on plantations in America, had probably done much the same.

* * *

Along with religion, politics defines small island life and party allegiances were fierce. There were two political parties, separated more by personalities than policies; the Peoples' Democratic Movement, PDM, which was in power when I first visited the islands and the Peoples National Party, PNP, which replaced them while I was at the Tourist Board. With an underlying resentment of their dependent status exacerbated by the often patronising attitude of the British administrators both parties wanted more independence from the UK. The PDM version was to have complete political freedom while expecting the UK to continue to pick up all the costs, a relationship which would have been pretty much the opposite of the 'taxation without representation' which had led to the American revolution; PNP saw that financial independence had to come first and when it came it would lead naturally to greater autonomy. Early in the Mokoro study I had been struck by how much people wanted me to know their political affiliation: taxi drivers the world over have political opinions but in TCI their political allegiance would be stated up-front. When I first met Big Louie, piratical-looking minister in the government at the time, he immediately showed me his chunky silver PDM ring, worn with pride.

Both parties, of course, had good and bad politicians, some capable, some incompetent, some dedicated and some corrupt – the politicians of my own country are no different. Being a small community I got to know most of them. The leaders of the two parties were polar opposites. Oswald Skippings, Skip, of PDM was short, squat, loud and abrasive, a demagogue and a bully who wore dark glasses and garish suits. Washington Misick, Washy, of PNP was tall, powerfully built, thoughtful and understated, an accountant-turned-politician who dressed rather more conservatively. I realised very early on that I had far more in common with Washy.

I enjoyed working with him when I was at the Tourist Board and he was Chief Minister and got to know him personally as a kind and considerate man. A few memories come to mind: he liked to use both Richard and me as impartial and objective sounding boards; one evening he wanted to throw a few ideas around informally and invited me to supper at the house he was renting, looking out over the sea towards the north end of the island. He rarely drank but on that occasion to unwind from the stresses of the day he had a rum and I had a beer as we watched the sun set. While on Grand Turk he lived on his own, his wife Trina staying at their home on Provo, and he had prepared a light supper. I was touched that he had included a starter of pickled herring - I had once told him that for a time I had lived in Copenhagen and enjoyed Danish food; such international delicacies were impossible to find on Grand Turk and he had bought it specially for me before flying over from Provo. Years later I was having supper with him and Trina and made the light-hearted comment that accountants, like me, were usually categorised as boring: Trina cut in: 'that's you, Washy, you're an accountant and you're boring!' She is now his ex-wife.

A mutual friend Patricia, who I first met on the dance floor of the Ramada early on in my time at the tourist board, now living in Cambridge but at the time on Provo, knew him much better. She told me that she was once at a lunch party with him when they saw a toddler about to fall into an empty swimming pool: with lightning fast reactions Washy dived across the corner of the pool to save it. Skip, I suspect, would have sat back and watched the child fall.

I got to know Washy's brother Mike when he became minister of tourism and I was at the Tourist Board. Some years later when he was back in opposition he discussed with me his long term business ambitions and I realised he wanted and expected to become a major player in the commerce of the islands. He took time off to get a law degree at Buckingham University; while he was there I met up with him and over lunch in London I realised that the boundaries between his commercial and his political ambitions were blurring. Shortly after he returned to the islands he in turn became Chief Minister, Washy having had enough of politics and returned to private life. I happened to be visiting when Mike took office; Gilley, a friend and a major PNP supporter, held a strategy-planning dinner for the new ministers and I was invited to join them. We sat till late in the night in Gilley's lovely house, high on the ridge with sweeping views south over the Caicos banks, discussing both the challenges and the exciting possibilities facing the new government. The previous PDM government had been drawn mainly from Grand Turk; now there was a government of ambitious young Provo-based men and women with private sector backgrounds and I was impressed with their grasp of the opportunities, TCI being by then well established in high-end tourism. But sadly some of them, having got their feet under the ministerial desks began also to get their fingers in the government tills and it became apparent that Mike saw his position as the opportunity to achieve his own financial ambitions. Eventually, accused of corruption he fled to Brazil where he was arrested and spent several months in jail before being extradited back to TCI. I last saw him being led to court under armed guard for his trial. At the time of writing the trial has been going on for more than four years; he is on bail and continues to live in comfort on Provo. He is reputed to be worth more than $100m.

* * *

For much of the time Grand Turk was a quiet, almost sleepy place with hardly anyone moving about much after nine at night, but occasionally it went into celebratory mood. Being the Caribbean there had to be an annual carnival but the one on Grand Turk fell some considerable way short of most others - fortunately expectations were never high. The first year I was there twelve floats were expected in the grand parade, five turned up, a couple excellent, the others drawing applause which was definitely more sympathetic than congratulatory. A small 'native village' had been built for the event, although the last 'natives' had left shortly after the arrival of Europeans 500 years earlier, and I spent the evening having a few beers with friends, both black and white (the friends as well as the beers - they served both Guinness and Corona). Socialising with the new Financial Secretary fresh out from the UK, with out-of-work Stacy, with the ambitious Nat, with the unfortunate drug-addicted Dale who spent his life wandering the island in an addled haze but was generally looked after by the community, and with the Governor I realised how integrated I was in the local community. Grand Turk is the sort of place where that is possible, quite unlike other places I've lived.

Shortly before I left the Tourist Board I went to a variety show in aid of the disabled, in the open air in the middle of town. The evening could only be described as balmy, a warm breeze drifting in from the ocean, the floodlit palm trees susurrating gently against the black night sky, the waves lapping the beach behind us. It was organised island style and ran on island timing; curtain-up was scheduled for 8.30 and happened at 10.15; there were two VIP guests, government ministers, both of whom were supposed to be presented with a bouquet of flowers; somehow one of the bouquets had gone missing so the other was divided up then and there and shared somewhat haphazardly between them. There were singers, mostly ranging from mediocre to bad but one or two with voices so beautiful they sent a shiver down my spine; there was one appalling stand-up comic who told some very off-colour jokes which seemed to amuse the ladies more than the men. Two teenagers, a boy and a girl, read a poem they had written for their father Don, suffering from muscular dystrophy and I was moved. The scheduled finishing time of midnight came and went. I left at one o'clock and was told the next day it had continued until gone two.

Later I got to know Don and his mother very well. Lenie was a few years older than me and divorced, short and stout with golden skin, curly white hair, twinkling eyes and a gentle sense of humour. She lived in a small white bungalow out on Hospital Road past Dot's Supermarket. Most of the time I lived on Grand Turk I was on my own and I took to visiting and reading to Don, who when I first met him could still speak well enough to be understood. I learnt that before he became ill he had been popular and gregarious but one by one his friends had stopped visiting, embarrassed by his illness. I did once persuade one of them to visit with me, to Don's obvious delight, but sadly the visits did not continue long. Lenie's house became one of my first ports of call whenever I returned to the island, and long after he had lost the power of speech Don would make noises of recognition as soon as he heard my voice. Lenie, with her warmth and kindness, was a great source of support as it became increasingly obvious to me that my marriage of 30 years had run its course; she had survived a difficult marriage herself. She was awarded the MBE in the mid-1990s in recognition of the service she gave as secretary to the Governor years before. Although she once told me that she would never accept an honour from the British (she had had little respect for many of the Governors for whom she had worked) she did fly to London to receive it. She nursed Don until he died, in the late 1990s, some ten years after his first diagnosis.

* * *

There were perhaps a hundred expatriates of European descent living on Grand Turk, some seconded from the UK and working for the government, a few in the financial services industry or running other businesses and a handful of wealthy long-term residents. Those of them who socialised did so mainly at the Saltraker and the Turks Head and I knew I could always find company there if needed. One of the Saltraker regulars was John Houseman, who was the spitting image of my father who had died a few years before I first went to TCI. He resembled him in looks and, to a great extent, in character and because I had never had a friendship with my father I was drawn to John, to his great surprise – most of the regulars ignored him. He had been in the islands for 25 years, as a hotelier and freelance journalist. Now he was retired but still writing, occasionally having articles published in quality US newspapers. He had had a distinguished wartime career in Greece and Burma, getting the Military Cross at the age of 18 while with the Special Operations Executive in German-occupied Crete. Like my father he was an excellent raconteur but unlike my father his stories had to be coaxed out of him, his default behaviour being surly and petulant. Among his exploits in Crete he had laid exploding donkey turds on the mountain roads, hopefully to destroy German vehicles, a peculiarly British way of waging war which suited John's eccentricity and sense of humour, sadly, as with my father, diminished by the ravages of alcohol. In a strange way John healed some of the hurt I felt over my relationship, or lack of it, with my father. I could talk to and drink with John as a friend and tell myself I was, vicariously, with Dad. He had been married several times and at one point took up residence, with his family, on East Caicos, the largest of the islands, uninhabited on his arrival and uninhabited once more after he left. Living with his last wife and his memories, he still published an occasional issue of the island newsletter Conch News which he had founded many years earlier.

John was in the Saltraker most evenings and Elaine kept a friendly eye on him and did her best to limit his rum intake. She and I had a minor falling out when she found I had bought him another drink after she had decided he had reached his limit. Looking back, there was something touching about the triangle: elderly alcoholic war hero getting drunk with a younger man; the younger man making up for the lack of a relationship with his dead father, with whom he never allowed himself to get drunk; and a bossy barmaid with the proverbial heart of gold looking out for the older man. With the Graham Greene-ish tropical island setting there's a one-act play in there somewhere.

The following year, terminally ill with lung cancer, John returned to the UK to die with the care he deserved, at the Royal Cambridge Military Hospital in Aldershot. My oldest daughter was living nearby at the time and at my request took him some flowers; she was his only visitor and the last non-medical person to see him before he died. To many of the short-term expats he was a little pathetic, a shrunken old man, living in his past, sitting drinking at the end of the bar. He was grumpy and irascible but also erudite and interesting. I always enjoyed his company and missed him when he was gone.

* * *

What little commerce there was on Grand Turk was limited to a few small shops, some of them calling themselves, with unjustified ambition, supermarkets, offering a very limited range to a captive market, dried and canned food supplemented by fresh fruit and vegetables whenever one of the sloops from Haiti had found favourable winds. Storage facilities were variable and I learned early on to be wary of anything frozen. One such 'supermarket' was Dot's, run by Dor and her husband Glen, who had a degree in economics from a minor university in Canada. They also owned a liquor store and were considered leading lights in Grand Turk's private sector. Glen had an opinion on everything and I would often pass the time of day with him, discussing local politics and the state of the economy. In one of our conversations, when his business was struggling, he said 'the problem with our islands is simple. It is one of money supply. They should supply us with more money.' TCI uses the US dollar as its currency and I believe he thought that all its financial problems could be solved if the Governor would only get the British government to send out more of them. Whatever he had paid for his college education was not money well spent.

Dor, in common with many on Grand Turk, was a large lady. I bumped into them once by chance in Miami and we went together to the Improv comedy club. A comedienne was telling some decidedly risqué jokes, loaded with inuendo, which Dor found far more amusing than Glen; Turks Island women seemed to me to have a more developed sense of ribaldry than the men. One of the jokes was about men with accents. Dor turned to me, slapped me on the thigh and said in her broad Grand Turk accent 'Das you, man! You'se gotta accent!' Where I come from my received pronunciation of the Queen's English, honed in a good British public school, is the norm. In Grand Turk I'm an oddity.

Life on Provo was very different to Grand Turk. The island, 25 miles long and up to three miles across, was considerably larger and its magnificent beaches had started to attract investment in tourism. The government bureaucracy on Grand Turk was unsure how to deal with the growing influence of American and Canadian entrepreneurs, so they were largely allowed to go their own way and their entrepreneurial spirit rubbed off on the local population to most of whom the cushion of a government job was unavailable.

I have always believed that it is possible to achieve success in life from any background. My maternal grandfather was born into a large family living in one of the poorest parts of London and died a millionaire, as did several of his brothers. When I lived in Africa I met a number of successful business people whose families were peasant farmers. TCI reinforced the belief that with application and a certain amount of luck most things are achievable.

Gilley ran the eponymous bar at Providenciales airport. Charming, handsome, sociable and efficient he was always there to serve the passengers on the handful of flights leaving the island. Gilley's bar, which offered a good range of food in addition to drinks, was one of the popular meeting places for locals. Gilley has an impressive air of natural authority and most of the tourists using the bar took him to be a very good barman without picking up that he not only ran it but also owned it. When I got to know him better he told me his story. At the age of 18 when tourism on Providenciales was in its infancy and he was only the barman he had got into conversation with an elderly American couple who were so impressed that they invited him to live with them for a while in the US. They arranged for him to go to college and he eventually graduated with a diploma in Hospitality and Culinary Management. Returning to Provo he bought the bar and continued to work there, putting in long hours and investing the profits in property. There were a couple of liquor importers on the island, both thriving because of the growth of the tourism industry but neither of them particularly efficient; Gilley saw an opportunity for some vertical expansion and began to import his own beer and other drinks. He negotiated the exclusive agency for Corona beer which became the most popular on the island, giving further impetus to his business. We would occasionally, in quiet moments, discuss his business and he once listed for me his assets, asking for my comments on his general strategy; his net worth by then was already into seven figures, not bad for a barman from North Caicos. In parallel his wife Althea built up her own successful business, a travel agency and secretarial bureau, later adding a rum bottling business, developing her own local brand. They are a handsome couple, both strikingly good looking and highly intelligent and I enjoy their company greatly. He served briefly, and reluctantly, as Premier in 2009, having forced the resignation of Mike Misick, but after a few months HMG stepped in and the local administration was suspended. He has since told me that he is relieved to be back full time in the private sector and to leave politics to others.

* * *

Although at times my life has required me to adopt a veneer of formality I much prefer the informal. I was returning to my house one Saturday morning with my arms full of laundry which I'd done in a friend's washing machine when I bumped into Washy, in shorts and tee shirt, helping a friend, one of our neighbours, to move house. We stopped for a chat, I elbowed aside Tiffany, a feral foal which had recently taken up residence in the compound, and continued on home. The incongruity of it made me smile: our respective status, by big nation standards, was Prime Minister and head of the Financial Services Authority. That's island life.

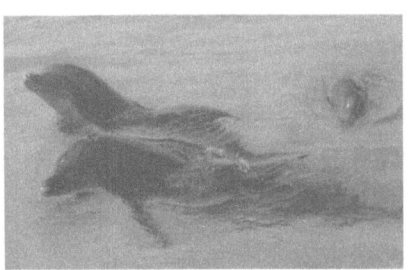

10. WHALES, DOLPHINS AND OTHER FISHY THINGS

I WAS PRIVILEGED TO SPEND nearly 10 years of my early adult life in East Africa where I discovered the pleasure of observing terrestrial wildlife. I watched rock hyrax sunning themselves on the rocks below the glaciers of Mount Kenya and green mambas draped in the trees of Gedi on the edge of the Indian Ocean. Between these climatic extremes I saw huge numbers of plains game and all 'the big five'. I also learned to scuba dive and had my first experiences of the extraordinary beauty of coral reefs and marine life. My time in the Turks and Caicos Islands has added to my store of wonderful wildlife memories.

When I first learnt that I was to visit the Turks and Caicos Islands I did some research at my local library and discovered that they were on the main migration route of the North Atlantic humpback whales. There are some five thousand of these impressive animals, 50 or more feet long and weighing up to 40 tons; they spend the summer months feeding in the rich cold Atlantic off the coast of New England and in October head south to the warm waters between TCI and the Dominican Republic. Here they stay for several months, gathering in large groups, mating and giving birth to the calves conceived the previous season. A few pass to the west of Provo but the majority travel through the Turks Island Passage separating Grand Turk from South Caicos. I recently told a friend that in TCI whales used to swim past my office: that was no exaggeration. It was not uncommon during the migration season to look out of my window and see the water spout of a whale blowing a mile or so offshore.

The first close encounter I had with whales was while I was Director of Tourism. A US based promoter (and as I later found out, con-man) had advertised a fairly expensive whale watching trip which attracted a modest number of paying customers. Apparently he told them all that one of their fellow guests would be Christie Brinkley, at the time a top fashion model. She later denied any knowledge of the promoter or the trip. He housed the group in the cheapest of the few hotels on Grand Turk and I was invited to give a welcoming talk, selling the very real attractions of the islands for nature tourism. The boat which the promoter claimed to have chartered never turned up so to minimise the adverse PR that this fiasco might give us I arranged for them to borrow the police launch, a powerful but not very comfortable 45' boat with very few seats. I joined them of course: I was not going to pass up my first opportunity to see whales swimming free, an ambition I had had since childhood from visits to the Natural History Museum in London where my sisters and I would gaze in wonder at the vast blue whale suspended from its ceiling.

We were about 15 people, one of whom, Mason, was a marine biologist who spent his life studying the humpbacks off the coast of New England. We headed for the Mouchoir Banks about 50 miles south of Grand Turk, accompanied by a group of bottlenose dolphins. After about thirty minutes Mason called out 'Whale breaching ahead!' I looked and saw, a few hundred yards in front of the boat, a solitary whale powering up from the depths till over half his body was clear of the water, the spray from his elongated flippers sparkling in the sunlight. He did this three times then disappeared. We carried on for another 20 minutes, then 'Whale on the right hand side!' It was a single juvenile, perhaps 20 feet long, which swam right up to the boat, its humped back carving smoothly through the surface of the water with little indication of the bulk below. When we got to the banks proper it seemed that the water was full of whales, although Mason told us we only saw seventeen in all. One time we were in the middle of a group of eight, apparently seven males competing for the attention of a single female. They were displaying, thrashing their long white flippers, diving, slapping their tails on the water and making porpoise-like leaps, not right out of the water but enough to show a large expanses of back. They were chasing and butting each other in mock battles and they were jousting, their tracks showing in lines of bubbles breaking the surface. A large male exploded through the surface no more than thirty yards from the boat, water cascading around him, his head, a huge part of the body, high above us. It was magic, a childhood dream fulfilled beyond all expectations. Just when we decided that there were no more around and the captain opened the throttle to head for home a big male surfaced right beside us, so close we could almost have reached out and touched him. His eye was the size of a soup plate and he looked straight at us for a few seconds. We called ourselves whale-watchers but as he slid back into his own world beneath the waves I wondered who was watching whom.

A few years later while visiting the islands for a holiday, I went out with friends to watch and photograph a group of whales just outside the reef off the west coast of Grand Turk, our little boat dwarfed by these huge animals, which ignored us lesser creatures. It was before the advent of digital cameras and I took many expensive photographs of the surface of the sea with a swirling disturbance the only evidence that a whale had shown itself a fraction of a second earlier, but I also got a few in which their Y-shaped tails were showing clear of the water. As we were motoring back to the island a light plane, forced by engine trouble to make an unplanned stop on Grand Turk, overshot the runway and finished up nose-down in the shallows, with only its Y-shaped tail sticking up out of the water; I can put two photos side by side and smile at the similarity. The young pilot escaped unharmed and insisted that one of our party dive down to rescue his brief case. He was en route from Atlanta to Columbia and to this day I wonder what was so important in the brief case.

The following day I went with my partner on a trip with Everett, one of the dive operators on Grand Turk. There were six of us in the boat and Everett knew and respected the whales, taking great care not to stress them. The first couple we found quickly disappeared but eventually we came across a mother with her new calf, making their lazy way north, in no hurry to trade the warm waters of the Caribbean for the rich feeding grounds of the north. We stayed with them for perhaps half an hour; she was aware of us and when Everett decided that she was sufficiently comfortable with our presence he signalled us to slip over the side, mask, snorkel and fins on. I did so, looked down and 10 feet below me, side by side, were the 40 foot long mother and her 12 foot calf. They appeared not to be swimming very fast but their leisurely movements are deceptive and I only managed to stay with them for perhaps half a minute before they faded into the distance, but it was a half-minute of transcendent bliss.

* * *

The seas around the Turks and Caicos Islands are also home to a large number of bottlenose dolphins, and during my time at the Tourist Board I came to know a remarkable couple, two best friends, one a man, the other a wild dolphin. One evening while relaxing in the bar of the Ramada I fell into conversation with a German photographer, Michael Friedel, whose photographs have been widely used to promote tourism in beautiful islands around the world. He had been commissioned to take photos of Jojo, a wild dolphin which had befriended Dean Bernal, one of the diving instructors at Club Med, the largest, and incidentally the least environmentally responsible, of Provo's dive operators. Jojo had been the youngest and smallest of a pod of dolphins stranded by the receding tide on the wrong side of a narrow sandbank just east of Providenciales. He was the only one to survive and it was fortunate that there had been people on hand who carried him back to the ocean. He was only a few months old when orphaned and initially he did not leave the sheltered waters along the North coast of the Caicos Islands; from the time he was rescued he looked to humans for companionship and it was rare to see him in the company of other dolphins.

Michael introduced me to Dean who always enjoyed talking about his friendship with the dolphin; I was a captive, and captivated, audience and the stories continued late into the night. He told me that not long after he arrived at Club Med he had been sitting on the sea-bed in shallow water, surrounded by the novice divers he was instructing when the young Jojo swam into the circle and introduced himself. This became a regular occurrence and bit by bit Dean became more involved with Jojo than he was with Club Med.

Jojo saw water-skiers as a challenge, a race to test him to the limits of his speed. At times Jojo would decide that no-one was going to learn to water-ski for a few days, so he would lurk beneath the Club Med pier and each time the novice skier rose from the water he would dart out and tip them over. Keeping company with divers and water-skiers had its dangers and he carried the scars of many a collision with a boat's propeller, scars which could and sometimes did become infected and which Dean treated with antibiotic paste.

In their play JoJo would take Dean, wearing a mask but without scuba gear, along the sea bed out to the reef, half a mile at around five knots with Dean holding Jojo's beak, or rostrum. He seemed to know intuitively when Dean needed to breathe and would bring him to the surface then take him down again. A favourite game was for Jojo to find a small nurse shark, drag it backwards by the tail until the reverse flow of water through the gills had half drowned it, then bring it to Dean for him to play with – Jojo liked watching Dean dance with comatose sharks. When the shark began to recover and become aggressive JoJo would insinuate himself between Dean and the shark and chase it off. I know, I know: as I recall and write this 30 years later it all sounds too fantastical but Michael had photo after photo of the two of them, human and dolphin, playing such games.

Dean had been in a relationship with a fellow American who became increasingly jealous of Jojo and the time that Dean was spending with him. She finally gave Dean an ultimatum: 'It's me or it's that fish' (marine biology wasn't her strong suit). Dean chose 'the fish' and she returned to the US. After a while he left Club Med and his easy-going dive-master's interest in a curious dolphin gradually evolved into a serious study of his friend; he decided to dedicate himself to the protection of Jojo and the documentation of his life. As his writing began to reach an international audience he became in demand as a participant at conferences on marine mammals, such participation taking him away from Provo, sometimes for extended periods. Returning from one such trip he went to the beach looking for Jojo – there was an uncanny telepathy between them and somehow Jojo, who ranged over many miles, always knew when Dean was around – to find that Jojo ignored him, swimming away when Dean approached. This continued for several days until Jojo, point made, could contain himself no longer and burst through the surface, turned a few summersaults and invited Dean, his absence forgiven, to come in and play.

During the decade or so of regular visits to TCI I usually managed to spend time with Dean. He based himself at Ocean Club where I used to stay when on Provo and I would seek him out at the end of the day to sit with a rum punch and listen to his stories while we watched the sun go down. He had his detractors, motivated I suspect by envy of his lifestyle and comparative fame, but I found him endlessly interesting. As I said I was captivated -

this friendship of a man and a dolphin was to last for many years and is well documented in videos and books.

Jojo had one other friend, a golden Labrador named Toffee, the regular crew of a yachtsman who took visitors out sailing. Jojo had an uncanny awareness of the whereabouts of his friends and would seek them out; Toffee, like most dogs a competent swimmer, would jump into the water and the two mammals, one marine and one terrestrial, would play happily together, Jojo the more agile and of course the more intelligent but Toffee having just as much fun.

I swam with Jojo a few times but never really interacted with him. The last time I saw him I was visiting with my family, sitting on the beach a mile or so from Ocean Club telling my daughters about this amazing animal when I saw movement in the shallows and there he was, in no more than three feet of water, watching us. We ran into the water, he flipped his tail and disappeared.

* * *

Bottlenose dolphins are the most common cetacean to be kept in captivity, trained to perform tricks for the amusement of humans. It is easy to anthropomorphise their facial features into a smile so humans continue to assuage their guilt at the mistreatment of these beautiful and intelligent animals by persuading themselves that the dolphins are happy living in a confined space and performing on command several times a day. They are not. Animal rights activists have long worked to raise awareness of this and the Born Free Foundation, established by the actor Virginia McKenna after making the eponymous film, decided to take the symbolic action of freeing a small number of captive dolphins to live in the wild. They were given sponsorship by the British newspaper Mail on Sunday who knew it would appeal to their core readership (who paradoxically are probably also the core market for dolphinaria) and possibly because of the attention attracted by Jojo they chose Providenciales as the ideal location for release. The waters enclosed by the crescent sweep of the Caicos Islands are shallow and teem with fish, the ideal place to train dolphins to hunt. As Director of Tourism I worked to help make it possible from our end.

A sixty acre seawater enclosure was built, separated from the ocean proper by large-meshed netting which allowed fish to come and go but prevented the dolphins from heading out to the dangers of the open seas. Within this enclosure was a small holding pen, twenty feet by ten, where the animals could spend their first days acclimatising to tropical seawater, very different to the heavily chlorinated water in which they had lived most of their lives.

The first to arrive was Rocky, who had been captured off the coast of Florida as a pup and spent the next 20 years of his life in a dolphinarium in Morecombe in the north west of the UK, swimming in circles and performing several times a day to delight visitors; for this he was 'rewarded' with defrosted frozen herring. His audience no doubt gave little thought to the fact that this wasn't his natural environment and that he would have been considerably happier living with other dolphins chasing red snapper. He was flown from London to Provo by British Airways, in a large canvas cradle with attendants to rub lanolin on him and gently bathe him in seawater to keep him moist. I was with the team meeting him at the airport. I wanted to say he was a magnificent animal but it is hard for an animal to be magnificent when it is so thoroughly miserable. He was large, perhaps nine feet long, his eyes had a defeated expression (maybe I'm anthropomorphising now) and his dorsal fin was bent over by many years of swimming in circles in the confines of his concrete pool in Morecombe. Dolphins, like most cetaceans, are social and very vocal, using a wide range of sounds to communicate: Rocky had been mute throughout his lonely captivity.

From the airport he was taken on a flat-bed truck to Leeward at the eastern end of the island, then by boat out to the small holding pen where he was lowered into the warm sea, his first taste of real seawater since he was taken from his family many years earlier. It would have delighted the press photographers present if he had immediately leapt for joy but he didn't. He lolled around listlessly for the first day or so but as he was introduced into the wider enclosure with the natural inquisitiveness of his species he began to explore. Then began the long slow process of teaching him the skills necessary to survive and thrive in the wild. He had a dedicated team of divers and marine biologists to help him but there were major difficulties to overcome. He discovered live fish but initially saw them as things to be chased for fun, not to catch and eat and the chasing wasn't as simple as it should have been, his bent dorsal fin causing him to veer all the time to the right. Throughout his adult life he had been fed with frozen herring and other fish didn't appeal. Dead fish were lined up on the gunwales of the boat, herring, herring, herring, red snapper, herring. They were thrown to him one by one: herring, swallowed, herring, swallowed, herring, swallowed, red snapper, tossed aside, herring, swallowed. Rocky was not to be fooled. But gradually the proportion of herring to other species was reduced and he came to realise, as have many of us, that red snapper has much to commend it.

The next step was to teach him to catch live fish. Dolphins are powerful swimmers and with Rocky's new-found 60 acre freedom and rediscovered joie de vivre his swimming was slowly straightening his dorsal fin; however small fish are fast and elusive and if you are given ready-caught fresh fish why bother chasing wild ones other than for the fun of it? So his supply was gradually cut down, and at the same time fish were caught and released near him having had their tails cut off (animal rights activists are less concerned with the rights of fish) and after a few weeks he was fully self-catering, but still mute.

While this was going on two more candidates for release were identified, a female and a male, Missie and Silver, who had lived in captivity for 22 and 13 years respectively in Brighton in the South of England. (While checking facts on this project I came across a number of articles written by defenders of dolphinaria, which refer to the animals being 'collected' rather than captured; similarly I once heard 'hunters' in the US referring to 'harvesting' wild bears: it is sickening to hear these monstrous abuses of our power over other species being disguised by weasel words). Again I was at the airport to meet them and accompanied them out to the marine enclosure. Rocky had been enticed back into the small holding pen as the team had no idea how the three of them would interact. There were three divers in the water and hydrophones to relay any sounds to us on the surface. The two newcomers, both smaller than Rocky, approached the pen tentatively: Rocky watched them carefully for some seconds then rolled over onto his back, the universal sign of submissive acceptance. Missie and Silver leapt out of the water, returned to Rocky who righted himself then broke his self-imposed twenty-year silence, bursting into speech and song. It was one of the most joyous moments of my life and along with everyone else my tears flowed.

Training Missie and Silver to catch their own fish was considerably easier: Rocky became their teacher. They spent a few months playing and hunting as a small pack and were finally released into the open ocean. It took some days before they were brave enough to swim beyond the outer reef but after that they were off - the project had been called, appropriately, Into the Blue. There were occasional sightings of them, sometimes together, sometimes individually. Missie was seen several times with Jojo but he had for years preferred the company of humans and the friendship did not last.

Critics of the project, most of whom represented the dolphinaria 'entertainment' industry, had always claimed that they wouldn't survive in the wild: maybe they didn't, but having heard Rocky break his self-imposed silence and sing for joy on meeting the others and having seen them hunt and play in the warm tropical waters I am convinced that even a few months of freedom were preferable to another decade swimming in lazy circles in a chlorinated concrete pool for the entertainment of humans.

* * *

This was not my first personal experience of captive animals being prepared for release back into the wild. The Born free Foundation was set up by the actor Virginia McKenna in memory of Joy Adamson who had spent much of her life raising orphaned lions in Kenya, training them to fend for themselves in the wild. Living Free, the sequel, was filmed on Crescent Island in Lake Naivasha, sixty miles north of Nairobi and at the time I was a shareholder in the Naivasha Marina Club which owned the island. The island varied in size from 800 to 2000 acres depending on the seasonal fluctuations of the water level. When the water was low we reached it by wading along a short causeway, taking care to remove the leeches which always attached themselves to our feet, at other times by boat from the club. Throughout the couple of years of our ownership we went there most weekends. We visited several times during the filming of Living Free and my young daughters were allowed to play with the lion cubs, the real stars of the film. When the cubs first arrived they were six-week-old bundles of fur with the exuberance and playfulness of all kittens; by the time filming finished they were six months old and considerably larger. They would signify the end of playtime with a good-natured swipe of a hefty paw; unlike those of domestic cats a lion's claws are not retractable and after we had been given a few bloody tramlines down our arms we reluctantly gave up playing with them.

A few years ago I re-visited Lake Naivasha, now the heart of a huge cut-flower industry employing many thousands of people. Through the depredations of this industry the water level has fallen at least 10 feet, Crescent Island is no longer an island and the little Naivasha Maina Club where we had spent so many idyllic weekends is now an abandoned ruin marooned a hundred yards from the new lake shore. Joy was murdered a few years after the film was made, as in his turn was her delightful husband George, Joy by a disgruntled employee, George by poachers.

* * *

It is easy to love the marine mammals, less so the large fishes but in their own way they are just as interesting. A mile or so to the east of Grand Turk is the uninhabited island of Gibbs Cay, home to a large population of sting rays and I visited a few times. It is an easy assumption that fish have little intelligence and certainly no personality but I found, swimming in shallow water with half a dozen stingrays that they are all different, each having their own distinct behaviour and indeed personality. Some of them seemed to enjoy physical contact and would slide over my feet and ankles, while others would hang back, curious but still keeping their distance. Their cousins the eagle rays which I occasionally encountered on my after-work swim behaved very differently. Unlike sting rays they appeared to be solitary animals and would appear like wraiths at the very limit of my visibility, just close enough for me to make out the beautiful markings on their wings, their chunky body and large eyes and graceful movements making them seem somehow more mammal than fish. They would never come closer than four or five metres and if I tried to approach them they would disappear back towards the open ocean.

Most days when I was in the islands I would go for an early morning swim and such swims would always be accompanied by fish, from the tiny pilot fish leading me out to the reef to the sleek and curious barracuda interested in watching another species struggling to cope in the environment in which it moves so effortlessly. My youngest daughter Emma, then aged 12, visited for a couple of weeks towards the end of my time at the Tourist Board and on her first day we swam together, I with a mask, she without. I looked down: 'There's a barracuda!' 'Yeah, Daddy, yeah.' 'And a shark over here!' 'Of course there is', she said patronisingly. I was of course telling the truth; young barracuda and nurse sharks, both quite harmless but impressive-looking fishes, are common in the shallow waters around the islands.

* * *

Although I had learnt to scuba dive many years before, during my time working in the islands I never once went diving. Perhaps, being cursed with a typical Anglo-Saxon work ethic, I didn't want my subconscious mind to think I was in the islands for pleasure, even though it was always an enormous pleasure to be in the islands. Fortunately, on my many visits back to the islands since I finished my professional assignments there my work ethic has not raised its head and I have enjoyed the wonderful diving available, both on Grand Turk and Provo. I still have a tee shirt given to me nearly 30 years ago by one of the US dive magazines when, as director of tourism I had commissioned some adverts. I cannot put it on without remembering the wonderful marine environment around the islands which I have been privileged to enjoy.

11. THEIR MAN IN LONDON

WHEN I WAS GROWING UP the British Empire spanned the globe but by the early 1990s it had been whittled away to almost nothing and what were once great swathes of pink on our maps were now a few unconnected dots. These were the last handful of colonies which considered themselves, or were considered by Her Majesty's Government, too small to be independent nations, plus Hong Kong which under various treaties was due to revert to Chinese sovereignty in 1997. Collectively these last pink bits were the British Dependent Territories, eventually renamed the UK Overseas Territories as some of them were noticeably less dependent than others. A dozen of them had settled populations, the 6m of Hong Kong being by far the largest, Pitcairn with its 50 or so descendants of Fletcher Christian and his fellow mutineers the smallest. The list was completed by a handful of anomalies: the British Antarctic Territory, a vast quadrant-shaped slice of inhospitable land with its apex at the South Pole, temporary home to a changing population of scientists studying the rich polar ecosystems; the British Sovereign Bases in Cyprus, left over from the bloody conflict of the 1950s when that lovely island wrested its independence from the UK; Ascension Island, home to fewer than a thousand people who service the US air base and the BBC and Cable and Wireless relay stations and are denied the right of permanent abode at the insistence of the United States; and the British Indian Ocean Territory, the settled population of which, the Chagossians, had been forcibly removed from the islands, their home for nearly 200 years, at the request of the US government so they could build their huge military base on one of the islands, Diego Garcia. This was the worst abuse of human rights by any British Government in modern times. At the time of the forced deportations in the late 1960s the islands were mendaciously described in official correspondence as unoccupied apart from migrant workers and 'a few man Fridays', language indicative of the patronising attitude of HMG to its remaining colonial responsibilities; as recently as 2009 an official at the FCO used a similar description. With the empire long gone, British imperialist attitudes linger on in Whitehall: in addition to the tiny pink bits on British maps one of the last remnants of its Empire is the latent racism of the old guard at the Foreign Office.

In 1994 the Governments of those Overseas Territories having permanent populations set up the UK Overseas Territories Association, UKOTA, to present a united front in negotiations with HMG which over centuries had honed the practice of divide and rule to a fine art. The prime mover was Tom Russell, the London representative and one-time Governor of the Cayman Islands, supported by his counterparts from Gibraltar and the Falkland Islands. The Turks and Caicos Islands were, at Washington Misick's request, represented by Richard Stoneman who had by then moved back to the UK. Richard's workload in post-communist Russia was increasing and when Washington Misick and his PNP party lost an election to their rivals PDM he decided to move on. I had time available and was visiting the islands several times a year as a non-executive director of Turks and Caicos Banking, so Richard suggested to the Governor that I take over and so in 1995 I became the official UK Representative of the Government of the Turks and Caicos Islands. For the next 10 years my name was in the annual

London Diplomatic List, albeit on the penultimate page: the only organisations considered by HMG to be less important than its overseas territories being the League of Arab States, The Palestinian General Delegation and the enigmatically named Independent International Commission for Decommissioning.

There was no job description and the duties were not exactly onerous, largely limited to the regular monthly meetings, the occasional need to brief the junior Foreign Office minister dealing with the Overseas Territories and an annual reception in one of the magnificent public rooms at the Foreign and Commonwealth Office. For the representatives of Gibraltar and the Falkland Islands, both with covetous neighbours with whom HMG maintained ambivalent relationships, it was very much a full time job but for me it was largely a reason to keep in touch with TCI and to try to further its interests wherever I could. There were perks, of course. In addition to the FCO receptions the representatives were invited to the Commonwealth Day services in Westminster Abbey where, representing the last remaining bits of the British Empire, we had front row seats, and the State Opening of Parliament. This ceremony is a wonderful example of British pageantry but I remember it best for one small embarrassing moment. One year I met for breakfast beforehand with three of my colleagues, the representatives of Montserrat, the Falkland Islands and St Helena. As our taxi approached the Palace of Westminster through the very high security in place at the time we were stopped at a police checkpoint. Asked for our invitations I reached into the inside pocket of my coat, one I hadn't worn for many months and produced, with an appropriate flourish, the piece of card from therein. The policeman was unimpressed: it was a flyer from Ann Summers.

Being on the Diplomatic List I began to get letters addressed to 'His Excellency W E Samuel' and invitations to various social events, one of which was the Commonwealth Jewish Society Annual Dinner. I attended a couple and well remember the host, the late Greville Janner, asking the High Commissioner of each of the Commonwealth countries represented, in alphabetical order, to stand and identify themselves and my embarrassment at hearing 'And the High Commissioner from the Turks and Caicos Islands – where are you, your Excellency?' I was tempted to respond 'cowering under the table, where do you think?' but duly stood and accepted the totally undeserved applause. Incidentally it is one of the little-know inequities of the relationships of the UK with its overseas territories that they do not themselves enjoy membership of the Commonwealth so, among other things, they do not join all the members in laying wreaths at the Cenotaph on Remembrance Day: although far from the theatres of war they all had citizens who had lost their lives fighting for 'The Mother Country' but 'Mother' chooses not to recognise this.

On the serious side we worked hard to improve the lot of the 300,000 or so inhabitants of these small territories. They were not a homogenous group. The inhabitants of Gibraltar, the Falklands and St. Helena were very aware of their British links and relied on them for support of various kinds. In contrast those living in the Turks and Caicos, a small group of tropical islands stranded by the tides of history on the fringes of the Empire, had no understanding of or expectations from their 'Britishness': why would they? They were mostly the descendants of slaves brought to the islands when their loyalist British 'masters' fled the American revolution, abandoned when the settlers discovered how barren and infertile the islands were. Most Turks Islanders went occasionally to Miami for their major shopping and culturally they identified far more with the US than the UK. Of those few who sought and could afford higher education the majority went to inner city Florida colleges. They resented being governed by British administrators, accepting it reluctantly as the fate history had decreed for them, the only small benefit being that their roads were built by the British – I was told several times that the British were responsible for TCI's roads as if that were decreed by history and one of the most important reasons for maintaining historical links.

Television on the islands was from the US, with all that implies culturally. I was on Grand Turk when the 1992 Olympics took place and watched the opening ceremony on one of the major networks, I forget which. The commentator said 'now here comes the delegation from Madagascar!' drawing out the first and third syllable; 'Now who the hell knows where Madagascar is?!' Not only was the location of the world's fourth largest island unimportant to him but he appeared proud of his ignorance, which presumably he expected his audience to share: sadly, many of them probably did. To Europeans Americans are an enigma; most of them are undoubtedly kind, generous and hospitable people but there is a lack of interest in the rest of the world apart from places which impact the lives of Americans directly and, to be slightly cynical, places which the United States decides to bomb. America was largely populated by immigrants who made the decision to leave their homelands in search of a better life, and most of their descendants seem to have little interest in the places their ancestors left. I have several times asked acquaintances who identify as, say, Polish American where in Poland their family's roots lay, to be met almost invariably with a look which says 'why would I be interested in that?' And of course there is the feeling, shared by many in my own country, that their homeland is somehow superior to everywhere else. On one of our trips to TCI my wife and I took a few days off to visit her cousin living on the west coast of Florida. We had had the usual nightmare treatment from the US immigration system at Miami Airport, queuing for more than two hours which at the time was not unusual. That evening we were discussing travel with our hosts who had visited the UK earlier in the year; they complained that on arrival at Gatwick Airport they had been delayed for 20 minutes at immigration; I related our two hour plus experience at Miami, to be met with 'yes, but you're foreigners'.

The great cultural divide between the US and the UK increases the gulf in TCI between the governors and the governed and in our meetings with the UK ministers responsible for the Overseas Territories I argued that to give the youth of the territories access to tertiary education in the UK would be far and away the most cost-effective way of easing the problems of governance of the territories. It would expose a number of their better educated citizens, some of whom would achieve positions of influence after their return, to the governance of the UK which, for all its imperfections, still has much to commend it. I was told repeatedly that the cost would be too great, a ridiculous and typically penny-pinching argument: there would be at most a few dozen students but they would return to their home countries with a much greater understanding of what the UK was and how it worked. Eventually the logic of this was reluctantly accepted and Turks Islanders, British citizens as they are, now have access to UK universities on the same basis as 'real' British citizens. The benefits of this were eventually reduced by the introduction of university tuition fees but until the disaster of Brexit they also had access as citizens of the EU to universities in other European countries, in many of which tuition is still free.

Of course the benefits of a good university education weren't without their downside. While Mike Misick was studying for his law degree at Buckingham University and we met for lunch I realised that, as his horizons were growing so too were his ambitions and his knowledge of the finer arts of corruption. This is of course no reflection on Buckingham University, a fine institution which is now generous enough to host the Buckingham Literary Festival of which my wife is one of the organisers.

As the official representative of TCI I was occasionally asked to do things which were, frankly, well beyond my pay grade. Perhaps the most unusual example was when the Marine Biology department of Southampton University, holding a one-day seminar on tropical fisheries or something similar, asked me to give a talk on the fishing industry of TCI. I explained that I was an accountant not a fisheries expert but they had already scheduled a slot in the timetable for TCI and I was the only person they could find within a reasonable distance of Southampton who appeared to know anything about the islands. So I re-read the Mokoro Report and dredged my memory banks for conversations with my fisheries colleague Tony, which were usually at the Saltraker over a few beers, recalled mentions of demersals and large pelagics and conch and lobster, and gave a talk long and rambling enough to preclude any time for Q and A.

By far the most memorable experience arising from my honorary office as London representative was my participation in the 2002 Commonwealth Games held in Manchester in the UK. The TCI team was led by my old friend and one-time beach-front neighbour Rita, by now a senior civil servant in the Department of Sport and Culture responsible for managing the very small contingent of four competitors. Rita asked me to join the team in the opening ceremony to increase the numbers.

I arrived at the Games Village Hotel, met up with Rita and her colleague Julia and was given my 'TCI national dress'. The population of the islands is mainly descended from slaves and, having been at various times a dependency of Spain, France, Bermuda, the Bahamas, Jamaica and the UK, 'national identity' is not clear-cut and 'national dress' non-existent. A couple of years earlier the TCI government had felt the need to encourage the feeling of identity by creating a national dress, and commissioned the Head of Culture David, a ballet dancer recently returned from a couple of years dancing professionally in Japan, to design one. I assume David's artistic nature was satisfied with the result but it said absolutely nothing about Turks Island identity: it was a loose-fitting white satin suit with multicoloured hoops on the arms and very large black buttons down the front, of which only a dozen were ever made, in a limited range of sizes. Rita had guessed at my size from our encounters on the beach. I took it up to my room and tried it on with great and justified trepidation – Rita's memory obviously hadn't been that good. I not only looked like a pregnant clown but the trousers were several inches too long and had to be taken up if I were to avoid the very real danger of tripping up as I marched past the Queen.

I took a bus into town to buy needle and thread and although needlework is very far from my strongest suit I managed to shorten the trouser legs. I put on the costume, looked at myself in the mirror, had a laugh and a couple of very large gin and tonics and went down to meet the rest of the team feeling like an idiot, the only consoling thought being that, in the Athletes Village of the Commonwealth Games, it was most unlikely I would meet anyone who knew me. In the lobby I met Rita and Julia, two lovely, short, dark-skinned ladies wearing the female equivalent, white dresses with flouncy skirts with multicoloured hoops and they looked stunning. I stood between them, towering over them, a pale white thorn between two beautiful black roses and we set off for the stadium where we were the most photographed team in the games, our picture appearing the following day on the front page of the daily Games Newspaper produced for the participants, next to that of the Queen.

The ceremony itself was surreal, marching round a stadium in a white satin clown suit and my well-travelled Tilley hat, in front of 60,000 people including the Queen of England, cameras flashing everywhere, making occasional eye contact with someone sitting way back: this is impossible to explain but there were times when I locked eyes with a single individual and everyone else disappeared for a second or two and then the moment was gone. The ceremony finished with all the thousands of competitors from every country in the Commonwealth, dancing in the middle of the stadium, a happy multinational multiracial crowd, relaxed and joyful. It was a very special occasion the likes of which I, as a non-athlete, had never expected to experience. Unsurprisingly Team TCI, which has neither stadium nor running track, did not distinguish itself, only appearing in the television coverage when the javelin-thrower narrowly missed spearing his left foot.

* * *

Although I was officially representing the TCI government in the UK, communication with the local ministers was spasmodic at best. While the governments of some of the territories, the Falkands, Cayman Islands, Gibraltar and St. Helena in particular, understood the need to engage with HMG, TCIG did not and for much of my time as UK representative I worked largely in the dark. I did my best to promote the interests of Turks Islanders but my emails to the Chief Minister, the closest I got to a 'Diplomatic Bag', went largely unanswered. Generally I was left to do what I thought was best for the islands. During my regular visits to Grand Turk I would meet with the Chief Minister, the Governor and others and suggest actions we could take in London to strengthen the relationship. Being Caribbean Islands these meetings often had a degree of informality. One time I was visiting with my partner and on our last night we were staying at a small beach hotel on Providenciales. We returned late from an enjoyable dinner, it was a still, moonlit night, the beach was empty, the sea inviting and we decided to go skinny-dipping. Emerging from our ground-floor room, Pauline wearing only a sarong, me a kikoi, that wonderful multi-purpose East African wraparound, we heard, from the nearby bushes, a loud 'Pssstt!' and the then Chief Minister Derek, a gentle and unassuming man, emerged, wearing a dinner jacket and carrying a parcel. 'I heard you're going back to UK tomorrow, could you take this package for my auntie in Manchester please?' He had been to an official dinner, knew where we were staying (on small islands there are few secrets) and waited patiently for our return. So, Caribbean Chief Minister in dinner jacket hands package to

London envoy naked but for a kikoi, to be smuggled to elderly lady in the north west of England. As they say, you couldn't make it up.

During that visit I had called in to the library on Grand Turk where the shortage of books was obvious. I was by then involved in the UK book trade as a director of my family's business Foyles Bookshop and on my return I contacted a number of publishers and asked for book donations. Within days we had nearly half a ton of books cluttering up Foyles' yard which needed to be moved out. I spoke to Patricia who is never afraid to ask favours of people in a worthwhile cause; she used airline contacts left over from her days as a travel agent in Bahrain and persuaded a reluctant British Airways to ship them out free of charge. Their arrival on Provo was covered live on the local radio: for a bookseller it is very satisfying to see books so valued.

On another of my visits the day I returned to Grand Turk I was invited to a party. I drove to the house and as I got out of my car the Governor's official transport, the white London taxi, drew up beside me. The driver's face lit up – we were old friends as he doubled as barman at official receptions at the Governor's residence, Waterloo. He made the introduction excitedly: 'Misser Samuel, Misser Samuel, dis de noo guvner! Guvner, dis Misser Samuel!' The time when I had been working in the islands was long past and the new governor was mystified but the driver who I had known for years just assumed his Excellency would know who I was.

There were other governors who did know me. One, with a reputation for womanising and drinking had made himself so unpopular with the local population that he was given a bodyguard from the Special Branch of the UK Metropolitan Police. Under his tenure relations between the islanders and the British administration gradually broke down until there was a period of almost open revolt, and at the request of the private sector, which continued to thrive on Provo but feared for the consequences of the breakdown, Richard and I jointly wrote to the Minister of State responsible strongly recommending that he heed the petition to remove the Governor. A couple of weeks later I was visiting the islands with my family and one of my daughters, a very attractive and at the time unattached young lady in her late twenties, formed a brief liaison with one of the bodyguards. He was warned off: I was apparently considered by the Governor to be a dangerous subversive for siding with TCI against HMG. He left a few months later.

The discrete presence of British police on the island reminded me of another time and another place when British police, in that instance the traditional London bobby, were used less discretely to ensure that law and order were maintained, an incident now largely forgotten but which had all the makings of a comic opera.

The rump of the British Empire, as it was gradually dismantled during the three decades after the Second World War, included a few tiny colonies which were considered by the colonial powers in Whitehall to be too small to cope with independence. As the winds of change swept through Africa large new independent nations were created; in the Caribbean, where the empire on which the sun was setting included many small islands, each with its own culture and traditions, with inter-island rivalries strong, this wasn't so easy. One such small island was Anguilla, a 15-mile long spit of sand east of Puerto Rico, the top right hand corner of the Leeward Islands. The population at the time was little more than 5000 and its nearest neighbours were the US Virgin Islands to the west and St Martin, shared by France and the Netherlands who knew it as St. Maarten, to the south. In the late nineteenth century the British had decided that it would be more convenient if Anguilla were administered jointly with the nearest other colony, St Kitts and Nevis so a federation was created, against the wishes of most Anguillians. The far more populous St Kitts had a comfortable relationship with its much smaller neighbour Nevis; between them and Anguilla was mutual antipathy and sixty miles of sea. As part of the British plan to give independence to all its Caribbean colonies the federation became the Associated State of Saint Kitts-Nevis-Anguilla with full internal autonomy, administration being in St. Kitts. The Anguillans were not happy.

Things came to a head when St Kitts stopped delivering the Anguillian mail. As with many Caribbean islanders most of the population had relatives living in the UK, from whom they now found themselves cut off: the British administration failed to sort this out and the situation descended into farce. Anguilla mounted an invasion of St. Kitts, sending a small fleet of boats the sixty or so miles to collect the post by force and the Anguillian revolution was under way. The invasion was easily repulsed, but not before the post office had been attacked and the mail claimed, and the Anguillians returned to their little island, remaining in open revolt. The British finally flew out a planeload of London policemen who eventually restored order with no bloodshed. I was fortunate enough to spend some weeks in Anguilla working on a study similar to the one Mokoro had done in TCI, and read the locally published version of these events, which related that, on the arrival of the British forces 'freedom fighters took to the hills'; as the highest peak on the small island is less than 250 ft above sea level I thought that this was perhaps over-romanticising this whole rather comic episode. En passant I would say that I found the Anguillians quite delightful to work with and I certainly didn't detect any militant tendencies.

The complete opposite to the TCI governor requiring police protection was his successor John Kelly, a delightful Irish born career diplomat who realised that the relationship with the UK, by that time at a very low ebb, would only improve if he as its representative were seen by the population to be working on their behalf. During the four years he was Governor he developed excellent relationships with the islanders regardless of social status; he was liked and respected throughout the little nation. His grounds at Waterloo were maintained by men from the prison; through my wife's work with the prisoners I knew some of them and was always greeted warmly when I arrived for a meeting with the Governor, one of my first courtesy calls on my occasional visits to Grand Turk. The previous Governor had frowned his disapproval, John Kelly smiled. His wife Jennifer worked within the local community, encouraging handicrafts and education and between them they did much to repair the damage done by his predecessor. When they flew out of Grand Turk for the last time a band of prisoners serenaded them onto their plane with a calypso-style song they had written specially: I believe John had ensured that they had the real instruments, lacking when they had performed for my wife and me in the prison some years earlier. The position of governor in the small dependent territories has none of the glamour and status of the major diplomatic appointments but the actions of governors can have a significant impact on the lives of the inhabitants of those territories. John Kelly represented British governance at its best.

By 2005 the population of TCI had more than doubled since my first visit and, with a growing international profile the government decided that it needed a permanent office in London. They appointed a full-time representative, Tracy, a Turks Islander married to a London lawyer, and my official connection with the islands ended: it had started as a one-off consultancy assignment of 6 weeks and expanded into a hugely enjoyable relationship spanning fifteen years.

I continued to visit from time to time. One visit was a year or so after Grand Turk was devastated by a major hurricane and I drove round, seeing the evidence everywhere and marvelling at the randomness of hurricane damage. I went to the Brown Houses in Palm Grove where I had lived twenty years earlier: many were untouched but where I had shared with Big Tom and Tashy my lovely, warm, temporary home there was nothing but a pile of splintered wood no more than five feet high.

My most recent visit was with my new partner, now my

wife, Vivienne. We stayed first on Provo, in Patricia's beautiful house perched high on a bluff looking out over the ocean. The first port of call, in the golf buggy Patricia used for transport, was the supermarket for provisions, where I was greeted warmly by a couple of old friends from the civil service. In the evening we ate at the Shark Bite in Turtle Cove which has made recent appearances in a couple of books by Peter James and went on for a night cap at Baci, an Italian restaurant nearby, where we bumped into Gilley, who had recently been Chief Minister, and arranged to meet for dinner. Next morning we had breakfast with Washy, another ex-Chief Minister and a couple of days later returning on a ferry from a trip to North Caicos I had a chat with yet another ex-Chief Minister, Derek of the moonlight skinny-dipping encounter. I thought back to my first arrival in the Turks and Caicos 23 years earlier: the Shark Bite and Baci didn't exist, Derek was a customs officer, Gilley ran the bar at the small airport and Washy was an accountant with a real-estate business and political ambitions. I love small island communities.

After a week on Provo we flew to Grand Turk, arriving in the late afternoon at the old Kittina, reborn a few years earlier as the Osprey Beach Hotel. I was met by the new owner Jenny who used to run the Saltraker, and the waitress Ivy who had been running the Kittina restaurant when I first visited the island. The next morning when I entered the lovely outdoor restaurant which surrounds the pool and looks down the casuarina-fringed beach towards the brown houses where I had briefly lived, I was given a big hug from the other waitress Anna Mae who had once given me lessons in dancing to island rhythms. She said, in her sweet, shy way, 'Hi Misser Samuel! I heard you was back! And wid a noo woman!'

That may well have been the last time I visit TCI. I look back on the relationship I had with the islands with great fondness and also some bewilderment that it could have happened. It spanned a period of great transition for me. I had arrived just after my life had been turned upside down by the quite unexpected termination of my investment banking career, when I was living in an over-mortgaged house in the outer reaches of Surrey with my 30-year marriage slowly and painfully grinding to its inevitable end and my finances in tatters. By the time I handed over my London responsibilities to Tracy I was divorced, living in a flat in Southampton Row in central London busy helping to turn round the fortunes of my family's business and with my personal finances back on an even keel.

It had been an equally huge transition period for the islands. In 1990 their finances too were in tatters, they were heavily dependent on the UK with whom they had a very antagonistic relationship and they were hardly known to the outside world, with fewer than 50,000 foreign visitors a year. Fifteen years later the population had grown from 12,000 to 30,000, GDP had risen eightfold, the relationship with the UK had become one of co-operation rather than opposition, the islands were financially independent with a thriving up-market tourism industry and were visited by more than three quarters of a million foreigners annually.

I continue to take an interest in the affairs of the islands, of course. In a recent election Washington Misick, who had once again taken on the leadership of his party, was elected Premier (the title chosen by his brother Michael to replace that of Chief Minister) 30 years almost to the day since he was first elected. I was also delighted that an old friend Josephine Connolly is a once again a minister. I knew her well when she was Josephine Smith, an ambitious Salt Cay born entrepreneur in Grand Turk. I went to her wedding when she married another friend Joe who ran the TCI office of one of the major accounting firms; it was, undoubtedly, the 1992 wedding of the year in TCI, a joyous and exuberant coming together of a Caribbean and a Liverpool Irish family with the church on Provo full to overflowing and celebrations which continued late into the night. I was also pleased that the airline entrepreneur whose manager in Haiti had paid my departure tax has been nominated for the Legislative Assembly by the Governor, the first Haitian born citizen to be so honoured. The next few years promise to be interesting.

* * *

My wife and I sometimes watch on television a light comedy series set in the Caribbean, 'Death in Paradise', and I commented recently that it triggered fond memories. She of course had not known me at the time and said 'Oh yes, so you were a policeman in the Caribbean?' and I replied 'No, but I was once Director of Tourism on a small island there.' It still seems unreal.

12. LESSONS LEARNED

LIFE HAS A WAY OF tabruptly changing direction when you least expect it; my unplanned and unexpected visit to the Turks and Caicos Islands 30 years ago was one such turning point, in a life which has had its fair share of unexpected change. Until then I had spent my working life entirely in the private sector, accepting government as something I couldn't change while being as critical as most of its frequent ineptitude. The Mokoro study was my first direct involvement with the public sector and required me to think objectively about the complex relationships between government and business and how such relationships could be channelled to encourage rather than restrain the growth of economic activity. It is far easier to see, in a tiny nation, what specifically will drive growth than it is in larger and more complex countries, to see the individual trees and not just the wood.

There is a great gulf between public and private sector mindsets. Governments often appear to lack awareness of the absolute necessity for wealth to be created before the creation of wealth can be regulated and of course taxed. The private sector wants to get things done: the civil service is interested in following procedures. It values process above result, wanting to do things right rather than do the right thing. I first became aware of this fixation on process when I was a young articled clerk: a client needed a particular income tax form, a P 9. I called the local tax office on his behalf and asked for one. 'What you need', they told me, 'is a P 8'. 'And what', I asked, 'is a P 8?' 'It is an application for a P 9'.

In self-contained economies the very direct link between taxation, only sustainable when there is productive economic activity, and the ability of governments to spend money is not always apparent to the general public. In TCI in 1990 the link between wealth creation and government finances hardly existed, with most of what little money the public sector had to spend being made available, reluctantly, by the British Government. The Technical Cooperation Officers funded by HMG were in positions to effect change but many of them had little real commitment to development, interested only in serving their time and building their bank accounts without blotting their copybook. They did not attempt to work proactively with the private sector, with the entrepreneurs whose motivations and methods they found very suspect. There was no personal benefit to be had by attempting to stimulate growth in the economy; any such growth would lessen the country's financial dependency and eventually render them redundant. Some of the local civil servants, recognising that the government was the major employer on Grand Turk, saw their prime function as the creation of more civil service employment rather than the provision of efficient services. As an example, Mokoro recommended that for as long as there was a lack of qualified Turks Islanders, trained teachers should be recruited from other Caribbean countries: this met with fierce opposition from the Education Department which appeared to see its primary function as being the creation of jobs for Turks Islands rather than the provision of good education.

I have learned that those with the mindset of the public sector should not be involved in commercial activities. A prime example was Tony Blair's vanity project to mark the arrival of the new millennium, the construction, on a sweeping bend in the river Thames, of a vast dome which had no clear purpose. As the historic date approached all the London diplomatic envoys were invited to a presentation to tempt them to consider hiring the spaces within the dome to showcase their countries. As the UK representative of TCI I was invited; most legations sent a mid-ranking official, a luxury our one-man legation didn't have and out of curiosity I went along. There were perhaps a hundred attendees and the presentation was made by the lady responsible for marketing the project, flanked by two assistants, behind them a large plan of the Dome and its surroundings. She used a long pointer to indicate the various areas with comments like 'this area's jolly big', 'this is going to be really nice' and 'this area's going to be called -' then a loud aside to an assistant 'what's this areas going to be called, Jim?' To most of the audience it was risible and as one of the few Brits present I squirmed with embarrassment but I could see from her body language that she thought she had done a pretty good job. Her feigned enthusiasm coupled with her lack of preparedness would have been unthinkable in the private sector.

I have learned that there is a sclerosis within the civil service which impedes change. In TCI that was exacerbated by the network of personal relationships within the very small community. During the course of my work at both the tourist board and the offshore finance centre I came across civil service logjams: A's department required something from B's department but as A was not speaking to B no request was made. The lack of communication between the Tourist Board, with its malfunctioning computer, and the government's IT department was a case in point. In a small community the intervention of an unconnected third person C can break up such logjams.

Inevitably the most important lessons I learned were about myself. My life before TCI had been peripatetic and the communities to which I occasionally belonged, from boarding school to expatriate, were largely transient. TCI was my first real experience of being in positions of influence in a comparatively self-contained small community. I did not of course belong, but I participated in ways I had never done before. Becoming a participant in small-community life changed my understanding of my own skills and weaknesses. I had always considered myself a numbers person, reasonably skilled in matters of finance, not especially so in dealing with people. Living and working on Grand Turk where personal relationships are so important and having to find ways to use those relationships in order to bring about progress I found that I was as much a people person as a numbers person.

And early on when, daunted by Washy landing on me the task of preparing five-year projections for the economy of the islands, I learnt from the encouragement of my daughter that self-confidence is a great enabler.

These two pieces of self-knowledge, that I am in part a people person and that moving out of my comfort zone is both challenging and stimulating helped prepare me for the next major challenge which came along in my life, to restore the fortunes of Foyles Bookshop, my family's business, following the death of my aunt Christina Foyle. Foyles too, in its way, was a small and caring community and my aunt's approach to its governance had similarities to that of HMG towards its dependencies, but that is something I have covered elsewhere.

POSTSCRIPT

I HAVE WRITTEN MUCH OF this memoir during Covid-19 lockdown, intensely aware of the impact of government actions, and inactions, on our lives. In normal circumstances most people get on with life while government operates in the background, its actions only attracting headlines in the media if there isn't a current celebrity scandal of greater interest. Government inaction is either welcomed because life is simpler if the status quo is unchanged, or is the cause of complaint which we know will fall on deaf ears. In today's extraordinary circumstances the early inaction and the unwillingness to accept what most experts advised, caused untold numbers of unnecessary deaths and the headlines have been thick and black and powerful. Good or bad, government matters.

Caribbean nations used to be characterised as banana republics run by mendacious politicians but any such mendacity pales into insignificance beside that of the current government of the UK. As their ineptitude became increasingly obvious I thought in my concluding chapter I could find parallels between their mistakes and self-delusion and the incompetence of the colonial administration of 30 years ago: as the months went by with the death toll rising and error being piled on error that became impossible. So I conclude with the hope that when 'all this is over' an unbiased review of the pandemic will lead to those who made such poor and very deadly decisions being held to account and more importantly, to changes in the way we are governed; if not I really fear that our children and grandchildren will inherit standards of public life in this once-great country of which I am deeply ashamed.

There are powerful forces within the system which favour the status quo. The very obvious success of the strategy laid out in the Mokoro report which led to significant and unprecedented public/private sector cooperation clearly had some short-term influence on the ODA/DfID. They subsequently commissioned Mokoro to carry out a similar exercise on the island of Anguilla and a few years later funded a study to help commercialise the economy of St Helena, led by Richard Stoneman and involving the London Business School. Sadly by the time we did the St. Helena study the lessons learnt in TCI had been forgotten, our proposals met fierce opposition from the old guard at the Foreign and Commonwealth Office and our recommendations for developing the private sector to drive growth were largely ignored. Fortunately the private sector-driven momentum in TCI in the early 1990s was sufficient to lift the country completely out of its centuries-long financial dependency and to irreversibly alter both the mindset of its people and its relationship with the UK. My 15-year involvement with the Islands which had begun with my membership of a team carrying out a strategic review of the economy and ended as an appendix on the London Diplomatic List had left a mark of which I am proud.

ACKNOWLEDGEMENTS

FIRST AND FOREMOST, THANK YOU to the people of Grand Turk who, while initially treating me with the scepticism they rightly showed towards visiting British consultants eventually made me feel, temporarily, a part of their small and caring island community.

Many thanks to Richard Stoneman for introducing me to TCI, for reading and commenting on drafts of the early chapters and for reminding me of things which I had, surprisingly, forgotten.

I am indebted to the late Tom Russell, one time Governor of the Cayman Islands and co-founder of the UK Overseas Territories Association, for his guidance during my time as London Representative. Tom was a wonderful example of colonial governance at its very best. He invariably acted in the best interests of the countries in which he worked, he knew what he wanted to achieve for them and he knew how best to achieve it. He was kind, intelligent, diplomatic and determined and a delight to work with. I strongly recommend his memoir *I Have the Honour to Be* which should be required reading for all aspiring diplomats as well as students of the closing years of the British Empire.

Thanks to Sukey Cameron of the Falkland Islands, Albert Poggio of Gibraltar, Janice Panton of Montserrat, Keddel Worboys of St. Helena and others who sat with me on the UK Overseas Territories Association and made it such an effective and supportive organisation.

After my formal relationship with the Turks and Caicos ended I retained an indirect link through my membership of the committee of the United Kingdom Overseas Territories Conservation Forum, set up some 30 years ago as a coordinating body for environmental NGOs in the remaining British territories. A portion of the proceeds from the sale of this book will go to the Forum.

Thank you to those who bought my first book *An Accidental Bookseller* and encouraged me to carry on writing.

Thanks to Jamie Keenan for the design of the book, both the cover and layout. As with my Foyles memoir his cover has captured something of Grand Turk.

Thank you to Assistant Professor Hemath Kumar of National College, Trichy, Tamil Nadu for copy-editing my drafts and making helpful suggestions on format, grammar and punctuation. As a retired bookseller I understand why Foyles' best-selling book on English grammar is published in India.

And lastly thanks to Vivienne, for her constant encouragement and her critical editing. It is, as I have said before, a great joy to have a wife and partner who shares my passions, including my love of words.

www.ingramcontent.com/pod-product-compliance
Lightning Source LLC
Chambersburg PA
CBHW020106240426
43661CB00002B/50